Starting with Books

Starting with Books
An Activities Approach to Children's Literature

Emilie P. Sullivan

1990
TEACHER IDEAS PRESS
A Division of
Libraries Unlimited, Inc.
Englewood, Colorado

TEACHER IDEAS PRESS
A Division of
Libraries Unlimited, Inc.
P.O. Box 3988
Englewood, CO 80155-3988

Library of Congress Cataloging-in-Publication Data

Sullivan, Emilie P.
    Starting with books : an activities approach to children's
literature / Emilie P. Sullivan.
    xv, 159p. 22x28 cm.
    ISBN 0-87287-792-2
    1. Reading (Primary)   2. Activity programs in education.
3. Children--Books and reading.   I. Title.
LB1525.S848   1990
372.4--dc20   90-10787
                                                    CIP

CONTENTS

MUSIC, MOVEMENT, GAMES (*continued*)

INTRODUCTION

Objectives

The main purpose of children's literature is enjoyment, though it can also accomplish a multiplicity of other goals. During colonial times, the purpose of learning to read was to be able to read the Bible and know the word of God. But society's view of children has changed, and with it has come a change of emphasis in children's literature. Children still acquire knowledge and insights from literature, but children's literature published in recent times is less moralistic and didactic than that of the colonial period. The themes of current children's literature are broadly based and address a variety of contemporary subjects, as well as entertain.

Literacy is a major focus of public education. When children first enter the elementary grades, the curricular emphasis is on *learning to read*. Later, the emphasis shifts to *reading in order to learn*. Involving children with literature from their very earliest years is an enjoyable, positive way to foster the reading habit. Those children who enjoy reading will continue to read after their formal education has ended.

Research has shown a positive relationship between reading to children and the development of linguistic abilities, which are a prerequisite to reading. Reading to children also provides opportunities for the child to develop self-awareness and an understanding of others.

Story Selection

An experienced teacher will probably have little difficulty in selecting appropriate stories for his or her children. A beginning teacher may be less familiar with children's concept development and thus have difficulty identifying material within a child's range to understand and enjoy. Generally, children of age six and under (preschoolers) enjoy picture books and picture book stories that are relatively short in length. The narrative will take five, ten, or fifteen minutes to read. Stories that require longer reading time are often not appropriate for a single session and may be beyond the attention span of preschoolers.

Stories for preschoolers should be relevant to their likes and needs. Preschoolers enjoy tales about animals who talk and act like people. They like stories involving other children. They appreciate humor or events contrary to logic.

There is a tremendous variety of books available for young children. If you are in doubt about the suitability of a story for a particular age group, consult such references as the *Subject Guide to Children's Books in Print* (R. R. Bowker), *Children's Books in Print* (R. R. Bowker), or *Children's Catalog* (H. W. Wilson). A number of professional journals review children's books and are listed under "Teacher Resources" at the end of this chapter.

The author has used many of the books listed in the bibliographies in this book in her teaching of kindergarten and college classes. Each subject area in *Starting with Books*—bibliotherapy, art, cooking, drama, language development, music and games—is followed by an annotated bibliography of related teacher resources and children's books. After using the sample activities in each chapter, you are encouraged to apply these procedures to other literary works listed in the bibliography. The activities provided may also be used with other books of similar content. Keep in mind that some of the books cited are no longer in print, but have been included because they may be found in a school library or, perhaps, your own personal collection. Becoming acquainted with the children in the class and their interests or developmental skills is the surest method to tailor book selection to that class.

Keep three things in mind when selecting books to read to children. (1) Choose books that interest you and that you will enjoy presenting to the children. Your interest and enthusiasm (likewise, your negative feelings) are easily conveyed to the children. Try to present the children with a good model, someone who enjoys the stories along with them. (2) Be aware of book size and the size of the group you will read to when selecting books. While pocketbooks may be adequate when reading to one or two children, a larger book is more suitable for reading to an entire class. Small books with small illustrations that require close inspection are inappropriate for a large group of young children. Each child wants to see the pictures, but quickly displaying them around the group leads to discontent. (3) Be aware of the subtle as well as the obvious message that the story is conveying to the children. Is the story condoning inappropriate behavior? Does it limit the role of male or female characters or display stereotypes? Are the illustrations and writing in good taste?

Reading to Children

The act of reading a story or poem can communicate many skills. Not only does oral reading assist the development of language and listening skills, but it develops other prereading skills, including left-to-right and top-to-bottom sequencing, discrimination of word boundaries, sense of story, and attention span.

Prereading

You should read stories yourself before reading them to the children in your class. Read a story to detect any terms or concepts that may require clarification prior to or during the reading. For example, the story *Fortunately* by Remy Charlip (Macmillan, 1985) is enjoyable for young children if the word *fortunately* is clarified beforehand. Without such an explanation, it will take the children longer to comprehend the story and illustrations. Another example is Adelaide Holl's *The Remarkable Egg* (Lothrop, Lee & Shepard, 1968). Children will enjoy learning and using the word *remarkable*, but the concept requires explanation.

Seating

Before beginning to read a book, assemble the children near you in a comfortable, relaxed arrangement. Ask the children to sit so that each one can see you (the reader) and the book. A good arrangement is for you to sit on a low chair facing the children who are grouped before you in a semicircle on the floor.

Presenting the Book

Once everyone is settled, get the attention of all the children on yourself and the book. Focusing the children's attention on the book may be done by displaying the book or asking a question relevant to the story to stimulate interest. (Examples of these types of questions can be found in the "Before You Read" part of many activities in *Starting with Books*.)

Introduce the book to the children by reading aloud the story title, author's name, and name of the illustrator. If the title appears in large print on the cover, hold the book up and point to each word as you say it. Give the children a moment to view the cover, comprehend the title, and informally comment before proceeding.

Open the book to the title page and again read the information relevant to the title, author, and illustrator. Point to each word as you pronounce it. Encourage the children to say the words with you. One way to do this is to read the first few words of a title and pause to allow the children to say the rest. Attention to the names of the author and illustrator helps the children understand the source of a story. Pointing to the words when introducing a book reinforces left-to-right and top-to-bottom sequencing and discrimination of word boundaries.

Reading the Story

Hold the book in a comfortable position for you to read and for the children to see the illustrations. If you have difficulty reading print that is upside down, which you must do if you place the book squarely in front of yourself, try sitting slightly sideways to the group. Balance the book on your knee as you read. Avoid moving the book about. Remember to maintain eye contact with your audience. At the end of each page, allow adequate time for the children to see the pictures and comment on them informally to each other. Avoid interrupting the flow of the story by asking questions about the pictures or making excessive explanatory remarks. Most stories explain the pictures adequately, and this encourages the development of listening skills. If there is something in a picture that you think the children have missed, point it out to the children and see if they react by nodding their understanding or agreement.

Beware of unwarranted interruptions by the children. Do not allow one child or a few children to disrupt the story through inattentive, disruptive behavior.

As you read the story, do not point to the words on the pages. Usually these are too small to be seen by a group, and pointing to the words proves to be a distractor rather than a help.

Use tone of voice and facial expressions effectively. Match your pace and tone to the story. Let the children see your interest in the story. Peek around the edge of a page to see what is happening next; pause to add suspense at appropriate places; exchange looks with the children at mystifying events.

After You Read

Do not always require the children to follow up the reading of a book with discussion or an activity. The children will appreciate the reading of a story for its own sake.

Following the reading of a story, place the book on the library table or wherever it will be easily accessible to the children. Make it available for several days or a week. The children will enjoy examining the book on their own. If a new idea or term has been introduced in the story, try to use it with the children during their discussion or sharing time. This reinforces the meaning and will encourage the children to use the term themselves. When the children show a special interest in a topic, you may wish to read other related stories or make them available to the children.

Most Important

Try to make story time an interesting and enjoyable experience for all.

Poetry

Poetry, rhymes, and finger plays are important aspects of the literature program for young children. Many children come to preschool programs with an acquired knowledge of some traditional nursery rhymes. Preschool instructors can build on this experience and enlarge each child's repertoire of rhymes, verses, finger plays, and poems.

Poetry requires prereading and practice to be read effectively. For short poems and nursery rhymes, large posterboard-size illustrated charts are useful in creating involvement and interest. A large chart, printed neatly in 2-inch-high letters, encourages children to model the teacher's reading behavior, especially if these charts are placed prominently around the classroom and referred to occasionally by the teacher.

Poetry and rhymes can be used to relate to all kinds of events in an early childhood education program. Poems about seasons, the weather, or animals, as well as those about skills like counting and sequencing, add variety and interest to the young child's literary experiences. Young children particularly enjoy humorous or nonsense verses. Familiar tunes may inspire new words for an old song. For example, the tune of "London Bridge" can accompany a song about fall—"Pretty leaves are falling down...." Some poetry may be acted out.

Children, even those who are very young, should be encouraged to create their own stories, poems, and rhymes. Self-created literature may begin simply with single dictated sentence captions of artwork and progress gradually to dictated stories and language charts. Self-created literature can be an important motivational part of the early childhood literature program.

Aids for Storytelling

Storytelling for young children can include the use of a variety of visual and dramatic aids. These include hand puppets, stick puppets, flannelboard figures, dolls, pictures, flip charts, and the chalkboard. Many of these aids are mentioned in the activities in *Starting with Books*.

Hand puppets may be used to gain the children's attention at the beginning of a story. The use of stick puppets can involve the children in the storytelling or, later, in retelling the story.

Flannelboard figures are particularly effective for use by children in retelling stories or creating new adventures for the characters. Retelling stories helps develop the children's memory, sequencing skills, and language skills. After using flannelboard figures to tell a story, make the figures available to groups of children for their own use.

Flip charts can be created by drawing large, bright pictures on the pages of a spiral-bound art pad. The visual impact of the pictures can be increased by using fabric or other textured materials in the drawings. For example, a chick can be created out of yellow-tinted cotton; bits of straw can be glued to a barnyard scene. Flip charts should be large enough for easy viewing by the group. After a story has been told using a flip chart, ask the children if they want to dictate their own version of the narrative. Make flip charts available to the children for storytelling on their own. Encourage the children to create their own flip-chart stories.

The chalkboard can be a very effective aid in storytelling. To create a chalkboard story, think of a few simple illustrations that can be easily drawn and that will help tell your story. It is a good idea to start the story at a point when the main character is very young, about the age of the children in your class. (Keep in mind that the character will get bigger as time goes by.) As you tell the story to the children, sketch a few selected events on the chalkboard. You may want to ask the children to help you color or shade in figures, or provide details. Occasionally add a single-word caption and identify it for the children. Children enjoy chalkboard stories and will want to retell them, adding their own drawings.

Creating Your Own Stories

Young children are egocentric. Although they enjoy hearing a variety of stories, they especially like tales about themselves and familiar places. When creating a story to tell to children, keep in mind that personalizing the story for your group of children can add interest and enhance the children's self-concepts.

The plot of an oral story should be simple and straightforward so that it is easy for the child to follow. Any problem to be solved should be introduced early in the story. The events of the story should move along briskly. Generally, it is a good idea to resolve any problems and demonstrate to the children that good will triumph over evil, and that even the smallest child or animal can succeed.

As you tell your tale, feel free to use all of the storyteller's wares—gestures, inflection, pace, and volume. Pause at appropriate points to allow the children to be caught in the mystery or humor of an event.

Storytelling is primarily for entertainment, but it may also be used to enhance self-concepts, communicate values, or develop listening and language skills. Catchy refrains encourage children to join in and become involved in a story. Occasional questions that refer to an earlier event in the story stimulate attention. New words or concepts may be used within the story and defined in context clues, or the main idea of the story can support the meaning of a word, as in the book *The Remarkable Egg*. In this story, the word *remarkable* becomes meaningful to the children as a result of the theme.

When presenting an original story, be sure of the plot, sequence of events, and characters, but do not memorize a narrative. Try to tell the story in a natural, casual manner. Adapt the story to your audience and memorize only those chants or refrains that will enhance the story. Keep in mind that eye contact and facial expressions are important and help convey your enthusiasm to your listeners.

Teacher Resources: Book Selection, Literature, Storytelling

Included on the next several pages under the heading of "Teacher Resources" is a list of books that may prove useful in book selection, acquiring information about children's literature, or developing techniques for storytelling. Each entry has a brief statement about the contents of the resource and identifies the type of resource as selection, literature, or storytelling.

THE BOOKLIST
Chicago: American Library Association
Published twice monthly September through July and once in August. Books and other educational media are reviewed.
selection

Baker, Augusta, and Ellin Greene.
STORYTELLING: ART AND TECHNIQUE,
    2d ed.
New York: R. R. Bowker, 1987
A how-to book about storytelling that stresses the value of storytelling and how to select stories. Includes a bibliography.
storytelling

Bettelheim, Bruno. *THE USES OF ENCHANT-MENT: THE MEANING AND IMPORTANCE OF FAIRY TALES*
New York: Alfred A. Knopf, 1976; paperback Random House, 1977
Written by a leading child psychologist, this book explains the importance of fairy tales in helping children cope with psychological problems of growing up.
storytelling

THE BULLETIN OF THE CENTER FOR CHILDREN'S BOOKS
Chicago: University of Chicago Press Journals
Monthly reviews of current children's books.
selection

CHILDREN'S BOOKS IN PRINT
New York: R. R. Bowker
Published annually. Books are indexed by author, title, and illustrator. Lists some 50,000 titles in paperback and hardcover, also large-type editions.
selection

Cianciolo, Patricia Jean, ed. *PICTURE BOOKS FOR CHILDREN*, 2d ed.
Chicago: American Library Association, 1981
Identifies and describes picture books evaluated by the National Council of Teachers of English.
selection

THE HORN BOOK MAGAZINE
Boston: The Horn Book
Published six times a year, this journal contains reviews of current children's books.
selection

Huck, Charlotte S., Susan Hepler, and Janet Hickman. *CHILDREN'S LITERATURE IN THE ELEMENTARY SCHOOL*, 4th ed.
New York: Holt, Rinehart & Winston, 1987
History, types of children's literature, selection criteria, and information on how to use children's books in the classroom.
literature

Johnson, Edna, et al. *ANTHOLOGY OF CHILDREN'S LITERATURE*, 5th ed.
Boston: Houghton Mifflin, 1977
Stories and poems for children.
literature

Lima, Carolyn W., ed. *A TO ZOO: SUBJECT ACCESS TO CHILDREN'S PICTURE BOOKS*, 2d ed.
New York: R. R. Bowker, 1985
Bibliographic citations by specific subject of picture books.
selection

Lonsdale, Bernard J., and Helen K. Mackintosh. *CHILDREN EXPERIENCE LITERATURE*
New York: Random House, 1973
History and types of children's literature.
literature

MacDonald, Margaret R., ed. *STORYTELLER'S SOURCEBOOK*
Detroit: Neal-Schuman Publishers in association with Gale Research, 1982
Folktales and folk literature indexed by title, subject, and motif.
storytelling

THE NEW YORK TIMES BOOK REVIEW
New York: The New York Times
Weekly reviews of the latest children's books.
selection

Polette, Nancy. *E IS FOR EVERYBODY: A MANUAL FOR BRINGING FINE PICTURE BOOKS INTO THE HANDS AND HEARTS OF CHILDREN*
Metuchen, N.J.: Scarecrow Press, 1976
Summaries of children's books and suggested activities. Contains a section on interpreting literature through art and includes instructions for making various types of puppets.
literature

Winkel, Lois, et al., eds. *THE ELEMENTARY SCHOOL LIBRARY COLLECTION*, 16th ed.
Williamsport, Penn.: Brodart, 1988
Annotated listing of children's books and nonprint indexed by author, title, and subject. Periodically revised.
selection

Ziskind, Sylvia. *TELLING STORIES TO CHILDREN*
Bronx, N.Y.: H. W. Wilson, 1976
Suggestions for developing skill in storytelling.
storytelling

BIBLIOTHERAPY

Realistic Literature

A comparatively recent trend in children's literature has been the widespread publication of realistic fiction—books dealing with the myriad of problems facing young people in their daily lives. While enjoyment is still the primary purpose of children's literature, topics have been broadened to serve secondary aims of self-understanding and enlightenment. Juvenile books of the first half of this century often pictured childhood as a time of happy innocence where concerns were minor. Literature of the 1960s and 1970s recognized the many vital issues that face children. With improved communications and increased general awareness in society as a whole has come a broadening of the content of children's books to include issues that trouble children.

Solutions, Encounters, and Differences

Bibliotherapy is not a new term. It was coined over a half-century ago. However, the practice of bibliotherapy may be new to many teachers. Bibliotherapy is an approach to helping children with their personal problems through books. The intent of bibliotherapy can be twofold: (1) It exposes the child to stories about other children who have dealt with a problem or situation similar to their own, and (2) it broadens horizons for children who have never encountered certain problems. Stories may be about children themselves or animals who dramatize human situations.

Many young children have had to deal with the problem of sharing their parents' time and affection with a new baby. Reading or hearing a story such as Martha Alexander's *Nobody Asked Me If I Wanted a Baby Sister* (Dial Press, 1971) may help an older child understand his or her own feelings of jealousy. Through discussion of the story problem, an anxious sibling may be guided to understand the intense needs of an infant. The older sibling may be led to realize that he or she, too, may have a role in helping care for the new baby. A sense of pride in this new role may be established.

Stories used for bibliotherapy should have plausible solutions to problems or should show that problems can be dealt with and accepted, even if they cannot be eliminated. Stories in which a fairy princess makes things right by casting a spell are not suitable for bibliotherapy. Children need to see realistic situations in which positive coping behavior is demonstrated. They must understand that escape into fantasy will not solve a problem nor provide long-term relief.

Bibliotherapy should help the child gain insight into his or her own situation or that of another. Stories should help the child realize that he or she is not alone in a particular experience and that others have encountered similar problems and coped with them.

In Beth Goff's story *Where Is Daddy? The Story of Divorce* (Beacon Press, 1969) a little girl has difficulty accepting the changed status of her family. She feels guilty and responsible for her parents' divorce. A child in a similar situation might find relief in the awareness that his or her own feelings of guilt are not abnormal. Children who have never gone through a divorce can gain an understanding of a friend's experience. In Goff's story, the mother and grandmother help the child to accept the situation in a realistic way. The story does not develop the false hope that the parents will reunite and the family lives happily ever after.

Realistic fiction gives the child the opportunity to comprehend another's point of view. Barbara Hazen's *Why Couldn't I Be an Only Kid Like You, Wigger?* (Atheneum, 1975) is a story that explores the advantages and disadvantages of being an only child. While a boy from a large family imagines the delights of being an only child, Wigger is feeling lonely. This is a good story for illuminating the differences in family patterns. Although a child may not feel free to discuss his or her personal concerns with others, the child may be less inhibited about discussing the feelings and actions of a storybook character.

Books about the handicapped and books emphasizing the acceptance of differences should be included in the literature for the young child. The ideal time to develop acceptance of differences is before stereotypes become ingrained. Books about the handicapped can do more than show the handicapped child that he or she is not alone. These books can help other children learn about disabilities and understand situations faced by the handicapped. Children need to see beyond the inabilities or special needs of the handicapped to their worth as individuals.

Children who are having difficulty making friends or relating to others may need examples of how good friends respond to each other. Arnold Lobel's *Frog and Toad All Year* (Harper & Row, 1976) or James Marshall's book *George and Martha* (Houghton Mifflin, 1974) fill such a need.

Death of a pet or loved person is not an easy situation for a child to accept and understand. Stories like Judith Viorst's *The Tenth Good Thing about Barney* (Atheneum, 1977) or Charlotte Zolotow's *My Grandson Lew* (Harper & Row, 1974) may help the child comprehend the cyclical nature of life and the positive effects of good memories.

Bibliotherapy cannot solve all the child's problems of growing up, but it can offer psychological support and insight for a confused or temporarily disturbed child.

Therapeutic Books

Books appropriate for bibliotherapy are not in a category apart from other children's books. They are generally fictional stories that realistically portray people dealing with problems. Occasionally, books used in bibliotherapy contain factual information in a story format. Books such as *The Emergency Room* by Anne Rockwell (Carolrhoda Books, 1985) or Tish Sommers's *Big Bird Goes to the Doctor* (Western, 1986) give the child factual information in story form about anxious medical situations. A child who is fearful of visiting a doctor or the hospital may be soothed by knowing what to expect.

Criteria

Books appropriate for bibliotherapy should meet all the criteria for good fiction. These include (1) a well-developed plot, (2) a worthy theme free of didactic or moralistic tone, (3) believable characters, (4) an appropriate setting that is true to its time frame and location, (5) a writing style that reflects the language and usage of the period and characters, and (6) format features such as illustrations, which enhance the story for the reader.

Overview

In this chapter are suggested activities for use in bibliotherapy and an annotated bibliography. The bibliography lists resource books that teachers and parents may find useful in further understanding the concept of bibliotherapy and also lists children's books related to specific problem areas. All children's books on this list are appropriate for use with young children from preschool and kindergarten age through the primary grade levels. Younger children will enjoy having these stories read to them. Older children might enjoy reading these stories for themselves.

The children's books are appropriate for reading and discussing with children in a group setting or individually. Children may wish to respond to the stories by expressing their feelings about the thoughts and actions of the characters, or by explaining how they themselves might react in such a situation. It is hoped that these books will serve as catalysts in helping children express their emotions. Teachers and parents will need to be attentive, sympathetic listeners.

Activities

Byars, Betsy C. *GO AND HUSH THE BABY*
New York: Viking Press, 1971; Puffin, 1982
Will's busy mother asks him to mind the baby. Will tries to entertain the baby
until the mother brings its bottle.

Materials

- drawing paper
- crayons
- magazines
- scissors
- paste
- stapler

Before You Read

Ask the children if any of them has ever been asked to help mind a baby. If so, briefly discuss what was
done. Then tell the children that you will read a story about a boy who was asked by his mother to mind a
baby.

After You Read

Ask the children how babies are different from them. The children may suggest such things as "babies
don't have teeth" or "babies can't talk." Next ask the children to name things they can *do* that a baby or
younger sibling cannot. Then ask the children how they might help take care of a baby. Point out that the
boy in the story helped out by entertaining the baby until its mother got the baby's bottle ready.

After a brief discussion about how the children can help, pass out drawing paper. Tell the children you
want them to draw pictures showing the things they can do that a baby cannot. For very young children,
you may have them select and cut pictures out of magazines. Next, ask the children to draw or cut out pictures that show how they could help mind a baby.

As the children are drawing, stop by their places and caption the drawings for them using their own
words. When the pictures are finished, put them together into two booklets entitled "Things We Can Do"
and "How We Can Help."

Followup

From time to time, ask the children if they have had a chance to help mind a baby or younger child. Ask
them how they felt about it. Encourage them to have positive feelings about helping others.

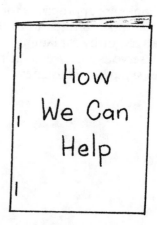

Feelings, Muriel. *MOJA MEANS ONE: SWAHILI COUNTING BOOK*
New York: Dial Press, 1971
Scenes of West African culture are used to illustrate Swahili counting words.

Materials

- poster-size sheet of chart paper (optional)

Before You Read

Ask the children if any of them knows how to count in a language other than English. If so, identify the language and ask the child if it was hard to learn. Tell the children that you are going to read a book about counting in Swahili, which is a language spoken in Africa. Tell them that after reading the story, you will all try to learn some Swahili words for numbers.

After You Read

Ask the children if they can remember the Swahili word for *one*. Say the word and have the children repeat it after you. If the children are able to read, you may wish to prepare a chart of the Swahili words and the equivalent Arabic numeral. If the children do not read, continue to teach the words orally. After the children have learned the first few Swahili number words, they may be able to use them in a simple number song or rhyme like "One, two buckle my shoe...."

Followup

Post the chart in the room. From time to time when you are talking about numbers, remind the children of the Swahili words for them. You may also want to read another book to them by Muriel Feelings—*Jambo Means Hello: Swahili Alphabet Book* (New York: Dial Press, 1974).

Mathis, Sharon B. *THE HUNDRED PENNY BOX*
New York: Viking Press, 1975
An old black woman, Great-great-Aunt Dew, tells young Michael about her century of living, using pennies to relate to historical events in her life.

Materials

- small box containing 100 pennies
- string
- tape
- magazines
- scissors
- crayons
- file cards

Before You Read

Ask the children if they have a friend or relative who is very old. Ask if that older person has ever told them stories about some event or incident that happened in that person's life. Tell them that this story is about a very old lady, Great-great-Aunt Dew, and her young nephew. Show the children the box containing 100 pennies and explain that each penny stands for one year in Great-great-Aunt Dew's life.

After You Read

Ask the children if they can tell some special things that have happened in their lives (e.g., getting a pet or bicycle, taking a trip). Next, tell the children that they are going to look through the magazines and cut out pictures of things that remind them of something they have done. When they have collected several pictures, they are to tape the pictures on the string to form a life line of events in order of occurrence. If they are unable to find the pictures they need, have them draw the events on the file cards using the crayons. They might also like to label their pictures. Later, have each child share his or her life events and hang the life lines in the room.

Followup

Have the children compare their life stories. Discuss how an older person's life line might differ in events.

Hughes, Shirley. *MOVING MOLLY*
Englewood Cliffs, N.J.: Prentice-Hall, 1979
Molly and her family move from a basement apartment in the city to a house with a yard. Everyone else is busy, so Molly plays by herself in the yard of the vacant house next door. When a family with twins moves next door, Molly, too, is busy.

Before You Read

Tell the children that you will read them a story about a girl who moved from an apartment in the city to a house with a yard. Ask them to think about what things might be different for the girl and what kind of problems she might have.

After You Read

Briefly review the book by discussing the differences between the girl's old and new homes. Then tell the children that they can play a game of old and new. Select one or two children to leave the classroom or cover their eyes for a few minutes. While they do so, have the other children make some noticeable change in the classroom, such as putting a table or chair upside down or having everyone stand in a line. Then have the children you selected guess what is new and different. Continue, if you wish, selecting others to guess the differences.

Lexau, Joan M. *EMILY AND THE KLUNKY BABY AND THE NEXT-DOOR DOG*
New York: Dial Press, 1972
As the result of her parents' divorce, Emily feels rejected and decides to run
away from home with her baby brother. She only gets around the block, but
her mother realizes the problem and begins to show her more attention.

Materials

- doll
- carriage or wagon
- clothing props
- drawing paper
- crayons

Before You Read

Ask the children to think about a time when they were unhappy and the reason they felt that way. Tell them that you are going to read a story about a girl who felt she had a reason for being unhappy.

After You Read

Ask for volunteers who would like to show how they think Emily felt when she ran away. One child may play Emily, another the part of the mother, and a third the part of the neighbor's dog. Encourage the children to use the props and let their faces show how they feel.

After the story has been acted out once or several times, have the children draw a picture of something that made them sad. As the children draw, stop by their places and label their pictures using their own words.

Next ask the children what happened to make them feel better. Encourage them to explain ways in which they did or could cope with their problems. Point out that these techniques can be applied when differences or other problems arise in the classroom.

Followup

Follow the same drawing and discussion procedure for those things that have made the children happy. You may want to list or draw pictures on the chalkboard to illustrate their responses as you discuss them.

Lobel, Arnold. *FROG AND TOAD ALL YEAR*
New York: Harper & Row, 1976
Frog and Toad are good friends who do many things together. In winter, they go sledding and drink tea. In summer, they have a funny experience with ice cream.

Materials

- magazines
- colored construction paper
- paste
- scissors

Before You Read

Ask the children to think about the things they do with their friends. Tell them that you are going to read a story about two good friends and what they do together.

After You Read

Ask the children how they could tell that Frog and Toad were good friends. Ask the children to tell other things that good friends do together or things that they do with their friends.

Distribute the magazines. Tell the children to go through them and try to find pictures of children doing the things that they themselves like to do. When the children have found and cut out enough pictures, have them mount the pictures on construction paper. Write "Things We Like to Do with Our Friends" on the paper and put it up on a bulletin board in the classroom.

Piper, Watty. *THE LITTLE ENGINE THAT COULD*
New York: Platt & Munk, 1976; paperback, Scholastic Book Services, 1979; Putnam, 1984
A train loaded with toys is unable to get over a mountain. Passing engines are asked to help, but refuse. Finally, one little engine agrees to try and succeeds while reciting the words "I think I can...."

Materials

- three or more large cartons with tops and bottoms removed
- tempera paint and brushes
- magazines, newspapers
- string, tape, scissors, glue
- large sheet of paper or poster board

Before You Read

Ask the children how they feel about trying to do something that seems very hard. Tell them that you are going to read a story about a little train engine that decided to try something hard.

After You Read

Ask the children what the little engine kept saying as it tried to pull the train up the mountain. Write the words "I think I can, I think I can" on the paper or poster board. Point to the words and have the children say them together, just as the little engine did. Ask the children why the little engine was unsure if it could pull the train over the mountain. Try to guide the children to realize the importance of trying to do a task even if it appears difficult.

Tell the children that they can make a train like the one in the story. Show the children the cartons and explain that one will be the engine and the others will be the cars containing the toys. Discuss with the children how train cars and engines look. Form the children into groups of two or three to paint or color each car. Wheels may be painted on or cut out of cardboard and fastened in place. While the train is drying, have the children cut pictures of toys out of magazines or newspapers. Then have the children glue or tape the pictures on the cars. Help the children attach the cars by poking holes in the front and back of each box and using the string. Finally, ask the children where on the engine they would like to put the "I think I can" sign and tape it in place.

Have one child get into each car and the engine. Have them hold up the cars and engine so that as they walk the train will move. Tell the children to pretend to be the train in the story. Lead the children in chanting slowly, "I think I can, I think I can ..." As they say the words, have them slowly walk and move the train toward an imaginary mountain. After they have gone over the mountain, they can say, "I knew I could, I knew I could ..." until they slowly stop the train.

Followup

Leave the train in the play area for the children to use. When the opportunity arises, remind the children of the little engine and the importance of believing you can do something difficult and then trying very hard to do it.

Raskin, Ellen. *SPECTACLES*
New York: Atheneum, 1968; paperback, 1972
Until Iris has her eyes examined and receives glasses to wear, she sees a world of strange creatures. She had not wanted to wear glasses, but changes her mind when she sees what a difference they make.

Materials

- pipe cleaners
- props to simulate a doctor's office
- play eye chart

Before You Read

If there are children in the class who wear glasses, ask them to describe how things look to them when they take their glasses off. Ask the children who do not wear glasses if they have a friend or family member who wears glasses. Ask them if they have ever looked through someone else's glasses. Point out that if they did, things would probably look different. Next tell them that you are going to read a story about a girl who saw strange things. Ask them to think about why she saw strange things.

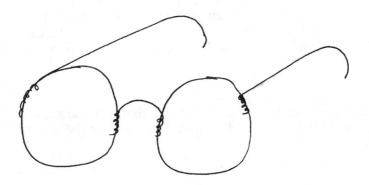

After You Read

Ask the children if any of them has ever had his or her eyes checked. After a brief discussion, tell them that they will pretend to have their eyes examined. Help the children use the props to set up a doctor's office. Ask for volunteers to make glasses out of pipe cleaners. Show them how to make circles for the glasses and how to bend the pipe cleaners to make ear pieces. Have the children connect the circles with a short length of pipe cleaner and attach the ear pieces.

When the glasses are ready, choose a child to play the doctor and others to be the patients. Show them how to use the eye chart. If the doctor recommends glasses, have the patient choose a pair of his or her choice. Have the children exchange roles as time permits.

Followup

Ask the children to collect pictures from magazines or newspapers of people who wear glasses. Point out that people in all walks of life rely on glasses. You might also like to read Patricia Giff's *Watch out Ronald Morgan* (Penguin Books, 1986).

Schulman, Janet. *THE BIG HELLO*
New York: William Morrow, 1976
A little girl and her doll, Sara, move to California. Everything is fine until
Sara becomes lost; then a new dog helps find Sara and a new friend.

Materials

- chart paper
- marking pen

Before You Read

Ask the children if any of them has ever moved. If so, ask if it was difficult to make new friends. Tell the children that you will read a story about a girl who moved to a place where she had no friends.

After You Read

Ask the children how the girl might have made friends if she had not lost Sara. Ask the children to suggest ways that they could help a new child in their neighborhood make friends. Stimulate discussion by asking the children how a new child might learn their names or what they like to do. As the children begin offering suggestions, tell them that you are going to make a list of their ideas. Ask the children what they think the list should be called. After the list is completed and titled, post it in the classroom.

Followup

From time to time, ask the children if they have had a chance to use any of the ideas on the list. If a new child enters the class, remind the other children how they can help the new child make friends.

Simon, Norma. *I WAS SO MAD*
Chicago: Albert Whitman, 1974
Many things that make children angry are described. Mother and Father say
it's not wrong to get mad—sometimes.

Materials

- chart paper
- marking pen

Before You Read

Tell the children that you will read a story about things that make some children angry. Ask them to think about whether the same things make them mad.

After You Read

Briefly review the story by asking the children if the things mentioned in the story make them angry too. Discuss the idea that anger is a natural emotion that adults and children feel from time to time. Then ask the children to make their own list of things that make them mad. You can write things down as the children suggest them. When you have ten or so items listed, ask the children how they might deal with their anger in each of the situations. The children may want to follow up this activity by making a list of ten or so things that make them happy.

Viorst, Judith. *THE TENTH GOOD THING ABOUT BARNEY*
New York: Atheneum, 1977
A boy is very upset when his pet cat, Barney, dies. His mother tells him to think of ten good things about Barney to say at the funeral. He only thinks of nine until he learns that Barney will become part of the soil and help the flowers grow.

Before You Read

Ask the children if they have ever had a pet that got lost or died. If so, ask them to briefly describe their feelings. Then tell the children that you will read a story that describes how a boy felt when his pet cat died.

After You Read

Ask the children if any of them has ever felt like the child in the story. Discuss their experiences. Point out that many people react in similar ways to such a situation.

Then ask the children if they know why the boy's mother wanted him to think of ten good things about Barney. Suggest that by making a list of good memories the child can help overcome his bad feelings about Barney's death. Ask the children if they can think of other ways in which the boy or someone else in a similar situation could overcome feelings of loss from death of a loved one.

Zolotow, Charlotte. *WILLIAM'S DOLL*
New York: Harper & Row, 1972
William wanted a doll, but his father and others did not want him to have it.
He was called a sissy. His grandmother solves the problem by getting him a
doll and explaining that William is practicing to be a father.

Before You Read

Ask the children if there has ever been a toy that they wanted badly but did not get. Discuss the various reasons why they did not get it (e.g., it was too expensive, it could be dangerous, it was not "suitable"). Tell the children that you are going to read a story about a boy who wanted a toy that his father and some others did not think he should have.

After You Read

Discuss with the children the varieties of dolls that are available or that have been popular throughout history. Help the children realize that dolls have been popular with both sexes.

Ask the children to think about their favorite toys. Tell them that they are going to play a game in which the object is to guess what kind of toy each child is playing with. You start the game by telling the children to make believe that you have a lump of invisible clay that can be shaped into any toy you wish. Then use your hands to shape the clay into a simple toy, perhaps a ball. Show how you would play with the ball. Call on the children to guess what the toy is. After the toy has been named, let the children take turns demonstrating in pantomime their favorite toys while other class members attempt to guess. When each child is finished, he or she should pass the clay on to the next child.

Throughout the game, point out that many of us can enjoy the same toys and that toys such as bats and balls or dolls and books are appropriate for both boys and girls.

Followup

Have the children make sock dolls according to the following procedure. Refer to the drawings on page 20. (*Note*: This activity is suitable for first graders or older. Do not attempt to do this activity in a large group or in a short time. Allow three or more work sessions to complete this project for each group.)

Materials

- one adult-size solid colored sock per child
- cotton batting or other stuffing material
- large-eye needles and thread
- yarn for hair
- cloth remnants for clothing
- buttons or permanent marking pens
- scissors

Steps

1. Make a cut about 3 inches long beginning at the toe end to form the doll's legs.

2. Cut off the cuff of the sock about 2 inches above the heel, which will form the head of the doll. The cuff section will form the pieces for the arms of the doll.

3. Turn the sock inside out and sew the leg seams. Then turn the sock right side out so that the seams are on the inside.

4. Put stuffing in the legs, body, and head, and sew the doll's head closed. Help the children tie a string around the sock just below the heel to form the neck.

5. Cut the cuff section lengthwise so that there are two pieces. Sew one end and side of each piece, leaving one end open for stuffing.

6. Stuff each arm piece. Then sew the arms to the doll's body just below the neck on each side.

7. The doll's body should be complete. Using permanent marking pens, draw the doll's face. Or, sew buttons on the face. A few lengths of yarn folded over several times may be sewn to the head for hair.

8. Clothing for the dolls may consist of simple jump suits. Be sure to make the pattern large enough to fit over the doll. Cut identical front and back pieces. Cut a slit down the front of the jump suit to allow room to put the doll inside. Sew the arm, leg, and side seams. Dress the doll and sew the front closed.

Ashley
Caldwell

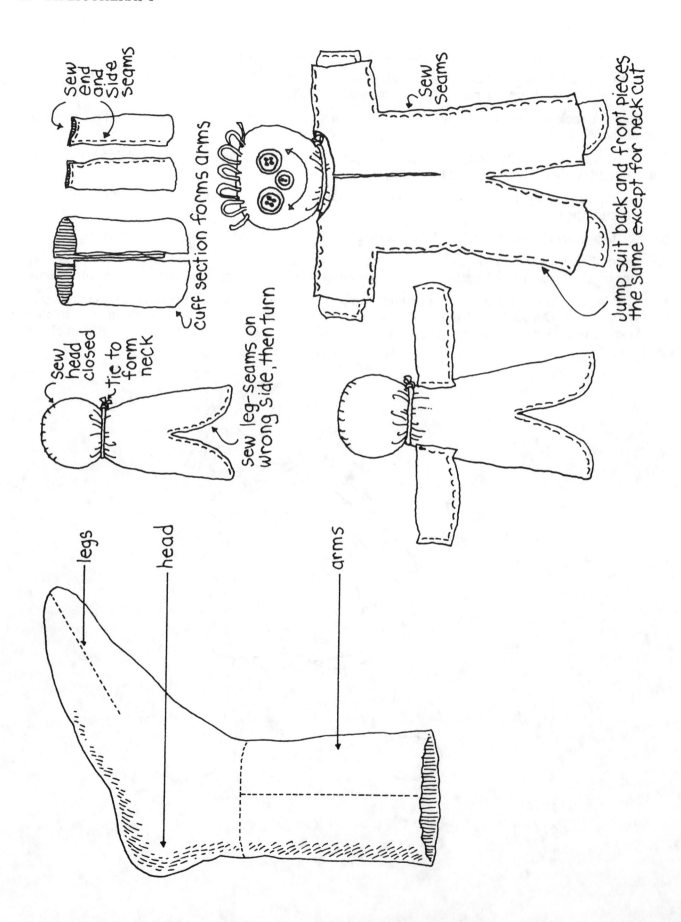

Sew end and side seams

Cuff section forms arms

Sew seams

Jump suit back and front pieces the same except for neck cut

Sew head closed

tie to form neck

Sew leg-seams on wrong side, then turn

legs

head

arms

Teacher Resources

Baskin, Barbara H., and Karen H. Harris.
*NOTES FROM A DIFFERENT DRUMMER:
A GUIDE TO JUVENILE FICTION POR-
TRAYING THE HANDICAPPED*
New York: R. R. Bowker, 1977
An annotated bibliography of fiction dealing with
the handicapped.

Baskin, Barbara H., and Karen H. Harris.
*MORE NOTES FROM A DIFFERENT DRUM-
MER: A GUIDE TO JUVENILE FICTION
PORTRAYING THE HANDICAPPED*
New York: R. R. Bowker, 1984
An annotated bibliography of fiction since the
early work.

Bernstein, Joanne E., (comp.) *BOOKS TO HELP
CHILDREN COPE WITH SEPARATION
AND LOSS*
New York: R. R. Bowker, 1977, 1983 (2d ed.)
History and aims of bibliotherapy. Includes an
annotated list of over 400 children's books dealing
with separation and loss.

Cornett, Claudia E., and Charles F. Cornett.
*BIBLIOTHERAPY: THE RIGHT BOOK AT
THE RIGHT TIME*
Bloomington, Ind.: Phi Delta Kappa, 1980
A paperback book on bibliotherapy.

Council on Interracial Books for Children
*HUMAN (AND ANTI-HUMAN) VALUES IN
CHILDREN'S BOOKS*
**New York: Racism and Sexism Resource Center
for Educators, 1976**
Describes a content rating instrument for human
values portrayed in children's books. Also reviews
and ratings of books.

Dreyer, Sharon Spredemann. *THE BOOK-
FINDER: A GUIDE TO CHILDREN'S LIT-
ERATURE ABOUT THE NEEDS AND
PROBLEMS OF YOUTH AGES 2-15*
**Circle Pines, Minn.: American Guidance Service,
1977, 1981, 1983 (vols. 1, 2, 3)**
Annotated bibliographies of children's books deal-
ing with specific problems of the young. Includes
subject and author indexes.

Fassler, Joan. *HELPING CHILDREN COPE:
MASTERING STRESS THROUGH BOOKS
AND STORIES*
New York: Free Press, 1978
Fassler, a child psychologist, reviews contemporary
children's books and suggests ways to use the
stories to help children cope with their problems.

Hynes, Arleen.
HANDBOOK ON BIBLIOTHERAPY
New York: Westview, 1985

Overstad, Beth, ed.
*BIBLIOTHERAPY: BOOKS TO HELP YOUNG
CHILDREN*, 2d ed.
St. Paul, Minn.: Toys 'n' Things, 1981

Rudman, Masha Kabakow. *CHILDREN'S LIT-
ERATURE: AN ISSUES APPROACH,
2d ed.*
Lexington, Mass.: Longman, 1981
Eight areas of current interest to youths are identi-
fied and discussed. Also has an annotated bibliography of adult and children's books for each category.

Stephens, Jacquelyn W.
*A PRACTICAL GUIDE IN THE USE AND
IMPLEMENTATION OF BIBLIOTHER-
APY*
Greatneck, N.Y.: Todd and Honeywell, 1981

Zaccaria, Joseph S., and Harold A. Moses.
*BIBLIOTHERAPY IN REHABILITATION,
EDUCATIONAL AND MENTAL HEALTH
SETTINGS*
Champaign, Ill.: Stipes, 1978
Includes a wide range of titles for use in biblio-
therapy.

Children's Books

Adoption

Caines, Jeannette Franklin. *ABBY*
New York: Harper & Row, 1976
A young child, Abby, enjoys hearing the story of her adoption. She has an older brother, Kevin, who is not adopted. Although Kevin prefers football to playing with Abby, he loves her very much and wants to take her to school for show and tell.

Girard, Linda. *ADOPTION IS FOR ALWAYS*
Niles, Ill.: Albert Whitman, 1986
A story format is used to give information about adoption and Celia's distress at learning she is adopted.

Gordon, Shirley. *THE BOY WHO WANTED A FAMILY*
New York: Harper & Row, 1980
Seven-year-old Michael, a veteran of foster homes, wants a permanent family and is finally adopted into a single-parent home.

Lapsley, Susan. *I AM ADOPTED*
Salem, N.H.: Merrimack, 1983
A simple fictional story about adoption designed for use with preschool or first-grade children.

Livingston, Carole. *WHY WAS I ADOPTED: THE FACTS OF ADOPTION WITH LOVE AND ILLUSTRATIONS*
Secaucus, N.J.: Lyle Stuart, 1978
Cartoon-style drawings tell the story of adoption and emphasize that adopted children are special and wanted.

Pursell, Margaret Sanford. *A LOOK AT ADOPTION*
Minneapolis, Minn.: Lerner, 1978
An informative book about adoption for young children.

Wasson, Valentina P. *THE CHOSEN BABY*
New York: Dial Press, 1971; paperback, 1977
This book is a classic in the field. The Browns adopt a boy and later a girl.

Death

Anders, Rebecca. *A LOOK AT DEATH*
Minneapolis, Minn.: Lerner, 1978
Using photographs and descriptions, this book helps to explain aspects of death to a young child.

Carrick, Carol. *THE ACCIDENT*
New York: Seabury Press, 1976
Christopher's dog Bodger is killed by a truck while they are out walking. The boy hates the driver of the truck and is filled with anger until he gets the chance to express his feelings.

Cohen, Janice. *I HAD A FRIEND NAMED PETER: TALKING TO CHILDREN ABOUT THE DEATH OF A FRIEND*
New York: William Morrow, 1987
There is a five-page introduction to the topic of death and how to deal with children. In the story a young child's friend is killed by a car; she asks questions of her parents about death, funerals, and so on.

Cohen, Janice. *JIM'S DOG MUFFINS*
New York: Greenwillow, 1984; paperback, Dell, 1986
A picture book illustrated by Lillian Hoban.

Coutant, Helen. *FIRST SNOW*
New York: Alfred A. Knopf, 1974
Lien's grandmother, who has come with the family from Vietnam, is slowly dying. Lien does not understand what dying means. As winter approaches their new home in New England, grandmother tries to explain death in terms of snowflakes, which melt and provide water for plants. Lien comes to understand and accept death as part of life.

DePaola, Tomie. *NANA UPSTAIRS AND NANA DOWNSTAIRS*
New York: Putnam, 1973; paperback, Penguin Books, 1978
Tommy calls his great-grandmother "Nana Upstairs" because she is always upstairs in bed. He calls his grandmother "Nana Downstairs" because she is usually downstairs cooking and keeping house. He loves them both and looks forward to weekly visits with them. One day the bed of "Nana Upstairs" is empty and Tommy sadly learns that she will never come back, except in his memory. When his grandmother also dies, Tommy thinks of both women as "Nana Upstairs."

Fassler, Joan. *MY GRANDPA DIED TODAY*
New York: Human Sciences Press, 1971
A boy describes his family's sadness at his grandfather's death and the things he used to do with his grandfather.

Grollman, Earl A. *TALKING ABOUT DEATH: A DIALOGUE BETWEEN PARENT AND CHILD*
Boston: Beacon Press, 1976
Written to help children understand death using the loss of a grandfather. A parents' guide provides suggested use of the book.

Harris, Audrey. *WHY DID HE DIE?*
Minneapolis, Minn.: Lerner, 1965
Unrhymed poetry. A mother explains to a young child why his friend's grandfather died.

Lee, Virginia. *THE MAGIC MOTH*
New York: Seabury Press, 1972
When Mary Ann dies after a long illness, her brother does not understand why she is gone. His mother tries to explain death to him. A moth emerging from a cocoon becomes a symbol of Mary Ann's spirit living on.

Miles, Miska. *ANNIE AND THE OLD ONE*
Boston: Atlantic-Little, Brown, 1971
In a Navajo village, an old woman nears death. She tells her granddaughter Annie that when a rug that Annie's mother is weaving is finished she, the Old One, will go to Mother Earth. Annie tries to prevent the rug from being completed until her grandmother explains the nature of life and death.

Ness, Evaline. *SAM, BANGS AND MOON-SHINE*
New York: Holt, Rinehart & Winston, 1966
Following her mother's death, Samantha pretends that her mother is a mermaid. Her father tries to get her to accept reality and end the "moonshine," or fantasy. Illustrations by the author won the Caldecott Medal.

Stein, Sara B. *ABOUT DYING: AN OPEN FAMILY BOOK FOR PARENTS AND CHILDREN TOGETHER*
New York: Walker, 1974
Death of a pet bird and later a grandparent are used to help young children understand dying.

Warburg, Sandol Stoddard. *GROWING TIME*
Boston: Houghton Mifflin, 1969
Jamie is troubled when his old collie, King, dies. His grandparents point out that even though King is gone his spirit remains with Jamie. His parents get him a new puppy to raise.

Zindel, Paul. *I LOVE MY MOTHER*
New York: Harper & Row, 1975
Flights of thought by which a little boy expands the realistic ways his mother loves him. Both mother and son miss the boy's father, who has died. Only in the final illustration is the mother seen, hugging her son, with the remembered father looming above them.

Zolotow, Charlotte. *MY GRANDSON LEW*
New York: Harper & Row, 1974
Lewis awakens in the night remembering his dead grandfather. He and his mother talk about his grandfather and decide that it is less lonely to think about him together.

Disabled

Arthur, Catherine. *MY SISTER'S SILENT WORLD*
Chicago: Children's Press, 1979
Although Heather is deaf, she enjoys her birthday party and a trip to the zoo.
deafness

Brightman, Alan. *LIKE ME*
Boston: Little, Brown, 1976
A child thinks about others and imagines that they are all much alike except for the rates at which they learn.
mental retardation

Brown, Marc. *ARTHUR'S EYES*
Boston: Atlantic-Little, Brown, 1979
Arthur is teased about his new glasses, but his improved sight soon helps him win the admiration of his schoolmates.
vision impaired

Cifton, Lucille. *MY FRIEND JACOB*
New York: E. P. Dutton, 1980
Jacob, an older boy, is retarded, but his young black friend understands him and helps him learn.
mental retardation

Fassler, Joan. *ONE LITTLE GIRL*
New York: Human Sciences Press, 1969
Laurie is a slow learner who has trouble doing her schoolwork. When her mother takes her to a doctor to be tested, she learns that some things will be difficult for Laurie, but that there are also many things that Laurie can do.
learning difficulty

Fassler, Joan. *HOWIE HELPS HIMSELF*
Chicago: Albert Whitman, 1975
Howie, who has cerebral palsy, attends a special school and uses a wheelchair. His wish is to be able to move the wheelchair by himself.
cerebral palsy

Jansen, Larry. *MY SISTER IS SPECIAL*
Cincinnati, Ohio: Standard, 1984
A story about a mentally retarded child.
mental retardation

Keats, Ezra Jack. *APARTMENT THREE*
New York: Macmillan, 1983
Following the sounds of a harmonica, two boys who live in a run-down city apartment building find a new friend, a blind man.
blindness

Kraus, Robert. *LEO THE LATE BLOOMER*
New York: E. P. Dutton, 1973
A young tiger named Leo has trouble doing the things his peers can do. Leo's father is worried, but his mother is confident that he will catch up with the others and he does.
learning difficulty

Lasker, Joe. *HE'S MY BROTHER*
Chicago: Albert Whitman, 1974
A small boy explains that his brother gets into trouble because of his learning difficulties, but he is still loved.
learning difficulty

Levine, Edna S. *LISA AND HER SOUNDLESS WORLD*
New York: Human Sciences Press, 1984
First, the senses of a deaf child are compared with those of a child with normal hearing. This is followed by the story of Lisa, who is deaf, why she cannot hear, how her parents helped her, and the special training she is receiving.
deafness

Litchfield, Ada B. *A BUTTON IN HER EAR*
Chicago: Albert Whitman, 1976
Angela often used to confuse things people said around her. When her parents realized her problem, they had her hearing tested. Now she wears a "button" (hearing aid). Nonfiction.
hearing impaired

Litchfield, Ada B. *WORDS IN OUR HANDS*
Niles, Ill.: Albert Whitman, 1980
This story is told by Michael of living with his deaf parents and how they communicate.
deafness

Montgomery, Elizabeth Rider. *THE MYSTERY OF THE BOY NEXT DOOR*
Champaign, Ill.: Garrard, 1978
When a new boy moves into the neighborhood, the other children think he is conceited because he does not return their greetings or talk to them. When they learn he is deaf, they decide to learn sign language. Chart of the signing alphabet included.
deafness

Montgomery, Elizabeth R. *"SEEING" IN THE DARK*
Easton, Md.: Garrard, 1979
Kay, who is blind, enters a new school where she must win friends and adjust to new surroundings.
blindness

Peter, Diana. *CLAIRE AND EMMA*
New York: John Day, 1977
Sisters Emma, age two, and Claire, age four, are deaf, but do many things together and are learning to speak. Photographs. Nonfiction.
deafness

Peterson, Jeanne W. *I HAVE A SISTER, MY SISTER IS DEAF*
New York: Harper & Row, 1977
An older sister tells about her deaf five-year-old sister and how she fails to react to noise.
deafness

Reuter, Margaret. *MY MOTHER IS BLIND*
Chicago: Children's Press, 1979
When a mother goes blind, she and her family must adjust to many changes.
blindness

Sobol, Harriet Langsam. *MY BROTHER STEVEN IS RETARDED*
New York: Macmillan, 1977
Beth, eleven years old, talks about her feelings for her mentally retarded brother.
mental retardation

Stein, Sara Bonnett. *ABOUT HANDICAPS: AN OPEN FAMILY BOOK FOR PARENTS AND CHILDREN TOGETHER*
New York: Walker, 1974; paperback, 1984
Separate texts for adults and children exploring the relationship between Matthew, a physically normal boy, and Joe, a disabled boy.
physical disability

Wahl, Jan. *JAMIE'S TIGER*
New York: Harcourt Brace Jovanovich, 1978
Nerve damage resulting from German measles causes hearing loss for Jamie. However, he learns to finger spell and use a hearing aid.
hearing impairment

Wolf, Bernard. *ANNA'S SILENT WORLD*
Philadelphia: J. B. Lippincott, 1977
The story of Anna, a child who was born deaf, and how her family helps her learn. Photographs.
deafness

Wolf, Bernard. *CONNIE'S NEW EYES*
Philadelphia: J. B. Lippincott, 1976; paperback, New York: Archway, 1978
Connie David, a girl blind from birth, acquires a seeing-eye dog, Blythe. Photographs. Nonfiction.
blindness

Wright, Betty R. *MY SISTER IS DIFFERENT*
Milwaukee, Wis.: Raintree, 1981
Carlo's older sister is mentally retarded. He often has to take her with him, but comes to see her special talents, too.
mental retardation

Yolen, Jane. *THE SEEING STICK*
New York: Thomas Y. Crowell, 1977
An emperor's only daughter is born blind, and he offers a reward to anyone who can help her. An old man teaches her to "see" with her fingers.
blindness

Divorce, Family Patterns, Working Mothers

Adoff, Arnold. *BLACK IS BROWN IS TAN*
New York: Harper & Row, 1973
The story of a close family in which the father is white and the mother is black.
interracial family

Alda, Arlene. *SONYA'S MOMMY WORKS*
New York: Simon & Schuster, 1982
A story about the adjustment that a little girl must make when her mother resumes working in an office.
working mother

Bauer, Caroline F. *MY MOM TRAVELS A LOT*
New York: Warne, 1981; paperback, Penguin Books, 1985
A little girl's mother travels a lot as part of her job, while the child stays home with her dad.
working mother

Blaine, Marge. *THE TERRIBLE THING THAT HAPPENED AT OUR HOUSE*
New York: Parents' Magazine Press, 1975; Macmillan, 1980; paperback, Scholastic Book Services, 1983
Everyone in the family learns to help out when the mother gets a job teaching.
working mother

Girard, Linda. *AT DADDY'S ON SATURDAY*
Niles, Ill.: Albert Whitman, 1987
Katie survives her upset at her parents' divorce and learns to have a good relationship with her dad, though they no longer live together.
divorce

Goff, Beth. *WHERE IS DADDY? THE STORY OF DIVORCE*
Boston: Beacon Press, 1969
A little girl has trouble accepting her parents' divorce and worries that her mother might leave as her father did. She learns to deal with her problems with the help of her mother and grandmother.
divorce

Hazen, Barbara S. *TWO HOMES TO LIVE IN: A CHILD'S-EYE VIEW OF DIVORCE*
New York: Human Sciences Press, 1978
Told from Niki's viewpoint; as his parents quarrel, separate, and divorce, and he comes to realize they will not remarry, he is loved in each home.
divorce

Hazen, Barbara S. *WHY CAN'T YOU STAY HOME WITH ME? A BOOK ABOUT WORKING MOTHERS*
New York: Western, 1986
working mother

Helming, Doris W. *I HAVE TWO FAMILIES*
Nashville, Tenn.: Abingdon Press, 1981
Patty and Michael learn to accept living in different homes with their parents after the divorce.
divorce

Lasker, Joe. *MOTHERS CAN DO ANYTHING*
Chicago: Albert Whitman, 1972
A picture book showing working mothers in different and nontraditional jobs.
working mother

Power, Barbara. *I WISH LAURA'S MOMMY WAS MY MOMMY*
New York: Harper & Row, 1979
Jennifer wishes her friend's mom were hers until the friend's mom becomes her sitter when Jennifer's mother goes back to work.
working mother

Schuchman, Joan. *TWO PLACES TO SLEEP*
Minneapolis, Minn.: Carolrhoda Books, 1979
David's parents divorce and he alternates living weekdays and weekends with his parents. His feelings of guilt and hope for the reuniting of his parents are dealt with.
divorce

Stanek, Muriel. *I WON'T GO WITHOUT A FATHER*
Chicago: Albert Whitman, 1972
Steve does not want to go to his school's open house because he has no father. However, his uncle, grandfather, and a neighbor go with him, and Steve is less concerned and self-conscious when he sees that other children do not have fathers present.
father absent

Surowiecki, Sandra Lucas. *JOSHUA'S DAY*
Chapel Hill, N.C.: Lollipop Power, 1972; 2d ed., paperback, 1977
A little boy who lives with his mother spends his day in a day care center.
working mother

Zolotow, Charlotte. *A FATHER LIKE THAT*
New York: Harper & Row, 1971
A boy idealizes the father he does not have. His mother tells him to remember that image and be like that when he grows up and is a father himself.
single parent

Emotions

Brown, Marc. *ARTHUR'S NOSE*
Boston: Atlantic-Little, Brown, 1976; paperback, 1986
Ashamed of his nose, an aardvark named Arthur goes to the doctor to see how he would look with another kind of nose. After considering many possibilities, he decides that he just would not be himself without his own nose.
self-concept

Fassler, Joan. *DON'T WORRY DEAR*
New York: Human Sciences Press, 1971
This shows young children that they will outgrow many of their problems like bed-wetting and thumb-sucking.
developmental fears

Kantrowitz, Mildred. *MAXIE*
New York: Parents' Magazine Press, 1970; reprint, 1980
Maxie is an old woman who always does things at a regular time. One day when she is tired she decides no one needs her so she does not get up, but she discovers that her friends are worried about her.
loneliness/aging

Mayer, Mercer. *THERE'S A NIGHTMARE IN MY CLOSET*
New York: Dial Press, 1968; paperback, 1976
A boy worries about a nightmare in his closet until he confronts it and overcomes his fear.
fear

Sendak, Maurice. *WHERE THE WILD THINGS ARE*
New York: Harper & Row, 1963; paperback, 1984
Sent to his room without dinner for being too "wild," Max conjures up a world of wild things in which he is king. Eventually, he returns to his room to find his supper waiting, and it is still warm.
rebelliousness

Williams, Margery. *VELVETEEN RABBIT*
New York: Doubleday, 1958; paperback, Avon, 1979, 1982; Alfred A. Knopf, 1985; Simon & Schuster, 1986
The velveteen rabbit is a Christmas present to a boy who quickly discards it on the nursery floor. Rediscovered later, it becomes a favorite toy. When the rabbit is old and worn, it is made "real" by a fairy as a reward for being a much loved toy.
love

Zolotow, Charlotte. *DO YOU KNOW WHAT I'LL DO?*
New York: Harper & Row, 1958
A little girl tells of all the fun things that she will do and share with her baby brother.
love

Zolotow, Charlotte. *THE HATING BOOK*
New York: Harper & Row, 1969
Because of a misunderstanding, two girls become angry with each other. The children remain angry until a parent intercedes to find the cause of the anger.
anger

Zolotow, Charlotte. *THE QUARRELING BOOK*
New York: Harper & Row, 1963; paperback, 1982
Bad weather makes a whole family cross until the dog makes Eddie laugh, and he passes on his smile.
anger

Zolotow, Charlotte. *THE STORM BOOK*
New York: Harper & Row, 1952
A bad storm is described as it occurs in the country and in the city. Mother holds her baby, and little brother sees the storm and later a rainbow. His mother assures him that the storm is over.
fear

Friendship

Blos, Joan W. *OLD HENRY*
New York: William Morrow, 1987
The story of an old man who moves into an abandoned house, and the friendship that eventually develops with townspeople.

Carle, Eric. *DO YOU WANT TO BE MY FRIEND?*
New York: Thomas Y. Crowell, 1971; Harper & Row, paperback, 1978
A mouse tries to find a friend among a variety of animals and eventually becomes the friend of another mouse. Wordless text.

Delton, Judy. *TWO GOOD FRIENDS*
New York: Crown, 1974; paperback, 1986
Duck and Bear and good friends. Duck, who likes things to be neat and clean, and Bear, who is a good cook, give each other special gifts.

Hoban, Russell. *BEST FRIENDS FOR FRANCES*
New York: Harper & Row, 1969; paperback, 1976
Frances, a badger, discovers that a little sister can also be a friend.

Marshall, James. *GEORGE AND MARTHA*
Boston: Houghton Mifflin, 1972; paperback, 1974
George and Martha, two hippopotamuses, are involved in a variety of humorous incidents that demonstrate the benefits of friendship.

Marshall, James. *GEORGE AND MARTHA ENCORE*
Boston: Houghton Mifflin, 1973; paperback, 1977
Each chapter shows how good friends feel about each other and how they demonstrate their feelings.

Marshall, James. *GEORGE AND MARTHA ROUND AND ROUND*
Boston: Houghton Mifflin, 1988
There are five short stories about the good friends.

Narahashi, Keiko. *I HAVE A FRIEND*
New York: Macmillan, 1987
A colorfully illustrated story of a little boy and his shadow.

Perkins, Al. *DIGGING-EST DOG*
New York: Random House, 1967
A lonely dog is bought from a pet shop and moves to a farm where he becomes depressed because he does not know how to dig like the other dogs. When he does learn, he gets into trouble, but his friend sticks by him. In rhyme.

Sharmat, Marjorie Weinman. *GLADYS TOLD ME TO MEET HER HERE*
New York: Harper & Row, 1970
Gladys and Irving are good friends who sometimes have disagreements.

Sharmat, Marjorie Weinman. *MITCHELL IS MOVING*
New York: Macmillan, 1978
When Mitchell moves away, he realizes he misses Marge and he writes her a letter inviting her to visit.

Van Woerkom, Dorothy O. *HARRY AND SHELLBURT*
New York: Macmillan, 1977
Tortoise and Hare, who are friends, decide to rerun the classic race. Tortoise wins again, but they remain friends.

Viorst, Judith. *ROSIE AND MICHAEL*
New York: Atheneum, 1974; paperback, 1979
Rosie and Michael are friends who play tricks on each other, but who also comfort each other in time of need and share secrets.

Zelonky, Joy. *MY BEST FRIEND MOVED AWAY*
Milwaukee, Wis.: Raintree, 1980
When Nick moves across the city, Brian is sad. However, when Brian later visits Nick, he realizes Nick has changed.

Zolotow, Charlotte. *MY FRIEND JOHN*
New York: Harper & Row, 1968
Two boys who are good friends share experiences.

Zolotow, Charlotte. *THE NEW FRIEND*
New York: Thomas Y. Crowell, 1981
A girl is upset when her friend takes a new friend in her place.

Hospitals

Hantzig, Deborah. *A VISIT TO THE SESAME STREET HOSPITAL*
New York: Random House, 1985
About the Sesame Street Hospital.

Hogan, Paula Z., and Kirk Hogan. *THE HOSPITAL SCARES ME*
Milwaukee, Wis.: Raintree, 1980
A story about the hospital.

Rey, Margaret, and H. A. Rey. *CURIOUS GEORGE GOES TO THE HOSPITAL*
Boston: Houghton Mifflin, 1966
George is a monkey who swallows a piece of puzzle and must go the hospital to have it removed. Hospital procedures are explained.

Rockwell, Anne. *THE EMERGENCY ROOM*
New York: Macmillan, 1985
An informational book about the hospital.

Sauer, Sue, et al. *STEVIE HAS HIS HEART EXAMINED*
Minneapolis: Univ. of Minn. Hospital & Clinic, 1983
An illustrated story about Stevie's hospitalization.

Shepard, Sue, et al. *COLOR ME SPECIAL*
Minneapolis: Univ. of Minn. Hospital & Clinic, 1982
A book about hospitals in story format.

Stein, Sara. *A HOSPITAL STORY*
New York: Walker, 1974; paperback, 1982
An informational book about the hospital.

Moving and School Adjustment

Aseltine, Lorraine. *FIRST GRADE CAN WAIT*
Niles, Ill.: Albert Whitman, 1988
Luke goes to kindergarten, but does not feel ready to go to first grade. He has trouble paying attention. His parents decide to let him stay in kindergarten.
retention

Chapman, Carol. *HERBIE'S TROUBLES*
New York: E. P. Dutton, 1981
Herbie is harrassed by a bully at school. He tries his friends' advice, but finally figures out his own solution.
bully

Cohen, Miriam. *BEST FRIENDS*
New York: Macmillan, 1971
Jim and Paul are friends, but this day, things go wrong and it takes cooperation to renew the estranged friends.
disagreements

Cohen, Miriam. *FIRST GRADE TAKES A TEST*
New York: Greenwillow Books, 1980
A placement test causes concern for first graders when a brighter child is transferred from their class.
testing

Cohen, Miriam. *NO GOOD IN ART*
New York: Greenwillow Books, 1980
Jim, a first grader, was discouraged from painting by a former teacher. It takes a new art teacher and classmate support to overcome his anxiety about art.
fear of failure

Cohen, Miriam. *WHEN WILL I READ?*
New York: Greenwillow Books, 1977; paperback, Dell, 1983
A boy continually asks his teacher "When will I read?" The ways children get ready for reading are explained.
school adjustment

Cohen, Miriam. *WILL I HAVE A FRIEND?*
New York: Macmillan, 1967; paperback, 1971
A boy who is beginning kindergarten is worried that he will not have a friend at school. His father assures him that he will make a friend, and he does.
school adjustment

Hogan, Paula Z. *SOMETIMES I DON'T LIKE SCHOOL*
Milwaukee, Wis.: Raintree, 1980
George has trouble with the arithmetic game and finds ways to hide his embarrassment until his understanding teacher helps out.
academic problems

Hughes, Shirley. *MOVING MOLLY*
Englewood Cliffs, N.J.: Prentice-Hall, 1979
Molly, an English girl, moves from the city to the country. She must adjust to the change and find new things to do.
moving

Locke, Edith Raymond. *THE RED DOOR*
New York: Vanguard Press, 1965
When Peter's family moves, he misses the red door to his bedroom. On his birthday, he discovers his new door has been painted red also.
moving

Rabe, Berniece Louise. *THE BALANCING GIRL*
New York: E. P. Dutton, 1981
A physically disabled child is pictured as a functioning part of a first-grade class. She deals with provocation from a classmate.
peer relations

Wolde, Gunilla. *BETSY'S FIRST DAY AT NURSERY SCHOOL*
New York: Random House, 1976
Betsy's mother helps her through her first day at a nursery school/day care facility.
school adjustment

Zolotow, Charlotte. *JANEY*
New York: Harper & Row, 1973
A girl is sad and lonely when she thinks of her friend Janey, who has moved away.
moving

Sibling Relations

Adler, Katie, and Rachael McBride. *FOR SALE: ONE SISTER—CHEAP*
Chicago: Children's Press, 1986
A story dealing with sibling rivalry.

Alexander, Martha. *I'LL BE THE HORSE IF YOU'LL PLAY WITH ME*
New York: Dial Press, 1975
Bonnie is younger and has difficulties getting her older brother to play with her.

Alexander, Martha. *NOBODY ASKED ME IF I WANTED A BABY SISTER*
New York: Dial Press, 1971; paperback, 1977
Oliver is jealous of his baby sister and tries to give her away to another boy. When the baby starts to cry, only Oliver can comfort her, and his feelings toward her change.

Arnstein, Helene S. *BILLY AND OUR NEW BABY*
New York: Human Sciences Press, 1973
Billy is jealous of the new baby and tries to get attention by acting like a baby himself. His mother builds up his confidence by pointing out the things he can do that a baby cannot.

Bach, Alice. *THE SMARTEST BEAR AND HIS BROTHER OLIVER*
New York: Harper & Row, 1975
The twins' parents understand the need for Ronald and Oliver to be different. They give the twins different presents and let each pursue his own interest—one in reading and one in eating.

Bonsall, Crosby. *THE DAY I HAD TO PLAY WITH MY SISTER*
New York: Harper & Row, 1972
An older brother tries to teach his sister hide-and-seek. When she does not understand, both are frustrated.

Byars, Betsy C. *GO AND HUSH THE BABY*
New York: Viking Press, 1971
Will entertains the baby while his mother is busy in the house.

Ferguson, Alane. *THAT NEW PET!*
New York: Lothrop, Lee & Shepard, 1986
The story of what happens to a household when a new baby arrives. It is told from the viewpoint of the house pets.

Grant, Eva. *WILL I EVER BE OLDER?*
Milwaukee, Wis.: Raintree, 1981
Seven-year-old David gets tired of his older brother's hand-me-downs and being compared with him. However, when he is away, the brother is missed.

Greenfield, Eloise. *SHE COME BRINGING ME THAT LITTLE BABY GIRL*
Philadelphia: J. B. Lippincott, 1974
A boy wants a baby brother, but when a baby sister arrives he is upset and jealous. His uncle explains that he felt that way once, too, and the boy comes to accept his role of older brother.

Hazen, Barbara Shook. *WHY COULDN'T I BE AN ONLY KID LIKE YOU, WIGGER?*
New York: Atheneum, 1975; paperback, 1979
A child thinks of all the advantages of being an only child like Wigger. At the same time, Wigger pictures the advantages of having siblings because he is lonely and surrounded by adults.

Hill, Elizabeth Starr. *EVAN'S CORNER*
New York: Holt, Rinehart & Winston, 1967
Evan wants a bit of privacy in the crowded family apartment in Harlem. He fixes up a spot for himself and also helps a younger brother.

Hoban, Russell. *A BABY SISTER FOR FRANCES*
New York: Harper & Row, 1964; paperback, 1976
Frances, a badger, is jealous of her baby sister Gloria and decides to run away. Hiding under the dining room table, she hears her parents talk of how much they miss her, and she decides to stay.

Hutchins, Pat. *TITCH*
New York: Macmillan, 1971; paperback, 1974
Titch, the smallest child in the family always has a smaller toy or part to play in things. However, he sows some seeds and grows a very large plant.

Jarrell, Mary. *THE KNEE-BABY*
New York: Farrar, Straus & Giroux
When a baby arrives, an older brother misses his mother's attention and the chance to sit on her knee. Later he gets his turn.

Keats, Ezra Jack. *PETER'S CHAIR*
New York: Harper & Row, 1967; paperback, 1983
When a baby sister arrives, Peter's old baby furniture is repainted pink. Unhappy, Peter decides to run away and take his chair with him. However, his parents make him feel better, and he helps them paint the chair.

Kellogg, Steven. *MUCH BIGGER THAN MARTIN*
New York: Dial Press, 1976; paperback, 1978
Henry is tired of being pushed around by his older brother Martin and dreams of becoming a giant. Henry's parents explain that he will grow in time and that Martin was little once, too. The boys become friendly, but when Martin resumes his bullying, Henry builds stilts and becomes bigger than Martin.

Zolotow, Charlotte. *IF IT WEREN'T FOR YOU*
New York: Harper & Row, 1966
A boy thinks of all the things he could have if it were not for his little brother. He later realizes that without his brother he would be alone with adults.

ART

Expression and Development

Art experiences provide children with opportunities to creatively express themselves while developing fine motor coordination skills and learning to follow directions. The activities that follow are designed to give children a chance to produce something uniquely theirs.

Although the children begin the projects with the same materials and some materials are precut, the child is encouraged to be creative. The focus is not on the child's completing identical or perfectly constructed products, but on the child's expression of his or her ideas artistically. Art activities should give the child a sense of accomplishment and pride. The actual activity, however, fills multiple needs and objectives for young children while remaining an enjoyable experience.

Simplicity

Beginning art activities with young children must be simple enough that all can be successful. The ability to draw comprehensible figures cannot be required of young children. Instead, art experiences can concentrate on the use of color, space, and materials in originals ways.

Early art projects often involve tearing and pasting pictures from magazines to form collages. Vegetable prints or finger painting are also very suitable for beginners. Painting with large brushes in bright colors at an easel gives children the chance to experiment with color and space. Clay and playdough provide children with experiences in creating three-dimensional objects and fill the young child's need for patting, pounding, and manipulating a material.

As children's motor skills and eye-hand coordination improve, increasingly complex art projects may be undertaken. Cutting and drawing activities require considerable skill development and control.

Overview

Following the activities in this chapter are teacher resource books and children's books related to art activities and holidays. Holidays often provide excellent opportunities for art projects, either to commemorate the holiday or mark a particular season of the year. Books listed under "Teacher Resources" should be helpful in finding activities appropriate to a variety of seasons and holidays.

Activities

Adams, Adrienne. *THE EASTER EGG ARTISTS*
New York: Charles Scribner's Sons, 1976; paperback, Macmillan, 1981
A rabbit family's job is to paint Easter eggs, but one little bunny does not
want to help. Then he discovers a new way to decorate eggs—with funny faces.

Materials

- blown-out egg shells, plastic foam egg shapes, or any egg-shaped container (one per child)
- tempera paint
- cotton-tip swabs
- string
- toothpicks
- small tree branch and container

Before You Read

Ask the children if they have ever painted faces or designs on eggs. Tell them that you will read a story about a family of rabbits whose job it was to paint Easter eggs.

After You Read

Briefly review the story by asking the children to describe how the bunny's egg designs were different from those of his parents. Then tell the children that you have eggs for them to design. (*Note*: If you are using real egg shells, you will have to prepare them ahead of time. To blow out the contents, pierce one end of the egg with a nail or ice pick. If the yolk is also pierced, the contents will come out more easily. Make a slightly larger hole in the other end of the egg. Blow through the smaller hole and the contents will come out of the larger hole. If the larger hole is about the size of a dime, and if the yolk is pierced, the contents may be shaken out of the egg. After removing the contents, wash the egg shells with water and allow to dry before painting.) If plastic foam egg shapes are used, a small amount of liquid glue should be added to the tempera paint to make it adhere to the foam. If plastic containers are used, permanent marking pens may be used instead of paint to decorate the eggs. A string loop may be taped to the egg to hang it. Explain step by step how to decorate the eggs.

Steps

1. Put on a paint shirt or smock.

2. Handle the egg shell carefully. Using cotton-tip swabs, paint a face or design on the egg. Be sure not to use the same swab in different paint colors, and put just a little paint on the swab.

3. To make a hanger for the eggs, tie thread around the middle of half a toothpick. Insert the toothpick into the hole at the top of the egg. When you pull on the thread, the toothpick will catch on the top of the egg and you can hang the egg by the thread.

4. Put the tree branch in the container, and hang the eggs on the tree branch.

Followup

You may also wish to read the following book to the children.

Milhous, Katherine
The Egg Tree
New York: Charles Scribner's Sons, 1950; paperback, Macmillan, 1981
Explains the custom of decorating Easter eggs and how to make an egg tree.
A Caldecott award winner. Cut out oval shapes from colored paper and decorate with crayon designs.

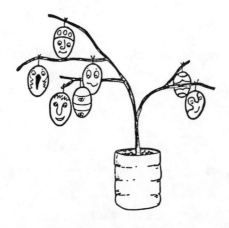

Armour, Richard. *STRANGE MONSTERS OF THE SEA*
New York: McGraw-Hill, 1979
Verses describe a variety of marine animals.

Materials

- sea shells, fossils, or other objects from which to make rubbings
- crayons
- thin paper

Before You Read

Ask the children to name some animals other than fish that live in the sea. Tell them that you will read a book about some of these animals.

After You Read

Briefly review the book by discussing the characteristics of the animals described. Then tell the children that they can make special drawings, called *rubbings*, of sea shells, fossilized sea animals, or other objects you have assembled.

Have the children remove the paper from the crayons they will use. Tell them to place a thin sheet of paper over the object they will make a picture of and rub the side of the crayon over the surface. The children may wish to exchange objects and make more than one drawing.

Carle, Eric. *HAVE YOU SEEN MY CAT?*
Matrick, Mass.: Picture Book Studio, 1987
While a little boy is looking for his lost cat, he sees many other kinds of cats.

Materials

- small paper sacks (one per child)
- construction paper for precut cat heads (see appendix A, page 126)
- construction paper scraps
- crayons
- scissors
- paste

Before You Read

Tell the children that you will read a funny story about a little boy who finds all kinds of cats when he is searching for his lost cat.

After You Read

Review the story by discussing the kinds of cats the boy saw. Tell them that you will show them how to make a cat puppet. You may want to assemble the puppet described below ahead of time to show the children. Explain step by step how to make the puppet.

Steps

1. Put the sack down flat so that the open end is toward you. Take a precut kitten head and paste it on the rectangular bottom section of the sack.

2. Draw a face on the kitten's head. Put on two eyes, a nose, and a mouth.

3. Cut thin strips of construction paper for whiskers and glue them on the face. Whiskers may also be drawn on the face.

4. On the side of the bag below the head, draw the cat's body and color it.

When the children have finished making the puppets, show them how to put their hands into the sack with the fingers bent into the bottom. By moving their fingers, they can make the head move up and down.

Followup

Have the children use the sack puppets in telling original stories about cats which they make up.

Bright, Robert. *GEORGIE*
Garden City, N.Y.: Doubleday, 1944, 1959
Georgie, a ghost, lives with the Whittakers in their New England home where he enjoys making the doors and stairs squeak. When Mr. Whittaker fixes the hinges and stairs, Georgie tries to find a new home until he learns that things have returned to normal at the Whittakers.

Materials

- white paper napkins or tissues
- marking pens
- string

Before You Read

Ask the children if they think there is such a thing as a ghost. Ask them what kinds of things ghosts are supposed to do to make some people believe they are real. Then tell the children that you will read a story about a ghost who makes noises in one family's home.

After You Read

Ask the children what kind of ghost they think Georgie is. Ask them if they think he would make a good friend. Tell them that they can make a little ghost like Georgie. Demonstrate how to make the ghost. Using two napkins, crumple one up into a ball and place it into the center of the other napkin, which should

be spread out. Bring the corners of the flat napkin together and tighten it around the ball. Tie a string around the covered ball to form the head of the ghost. You will probably need to help the children form the knot. Next, using the marking pen, draw a face on your ghost.

You may wish to use some of the ghosts as bulletin board decorations. Or, the children may enjoy using them in singing a ghostly song.

There are several other books written by Robert Bright about Georgie the ghost (one of them is *Georgie and the Robbers*). You might enjoy reading these to your class or placing them on display.

Carle, Eric. *THE VERY HUNGRY CATERPILLAR*
Cleveland, Ohio: William Collins & World, 1969; New York: Scholastic Book
Services, 1975; Putnam, 1981; miniature ed., 1986
The life stages of a butterfly through egg, caterpillar, and cocoon.

Materials

- spring-type clothes pins (one per child)
- tissue paper
- cardboard for butterfly wing pattern (see appendix A, page 127)
- scissors
- marking pens, crayons, pencils

Before You Read

Tell the children that you will read them a story about the changes a butterfly goes through while it is growing up.

After You Read

Ask the children if they can tell you the stages in a butterfly's life. Encourage them to describe the life cycle in the correct sequence. Use the pictures in the book to prompt responses.

You may wish to prepare the wing pattern and assemble one butterfly ahead of time. Show it to the children, and explain step by step how to make the butterfly.

Steps

1. Trace around the cardboard wing pattern on tissue paper.

2. Cut out the wings. (For very young children, you may wish to precut the wings.)

3. Draw a design on the wings. Work very carefully because the tissue paper is fragile and easily torn, just like real butterfly wings.

4. Gather up the tissue paper along the center and insert it into the clamping end of the pin. (You may wish to help young children put the wings on the pin.)

5. Draw eyes and body stripes on top of the closed end of the pin.

The children may wish to pin their butterflies to their collars. Ask them to tell their parents about the life of the butterfly when they get home.

Followup

Cut out butterfly shapes from colored wax paper and tape them to windows or hang them with string from light fixtures. Wax paper can be colored by painting it with tempera paint to which liquid detergent has been added. Or, use inexpensive pencil sharpeners to make crayon shavings of different colors. Sprinkle the shavings on a sheet of wax paper and cover it with another sheet of wax paper. Using a warm iron, iron the two sheets of wax paper together. (*Note*: Very little crayon or heat is needed.)

Carlson, Nancy L. *HARRIET AND THE GARDEN*
Minneapolis, Minn.: Carolrhoda Books, 1982
Harriet is playing baseball when she accidentally falls into Mrs. Hoozit's flower garden and breaks the prize dahlia.

Materials

- small pots, jars, or plastic foam cups (one per child)
- potting soil
- seeds
- pebbles
- rickrack or other trimming
- glue
- marking pens or crayons

Before You Read

Ask the children what kinds of activities take place in the spring. If none of the children mentions them, discuss gardening and baseball. Note that in the spring people often work and play out of doors. Tell the children that you will read a story about what might happen in the spring while playing baseball.

After You Read

Review the story by asking the children why Harriet was upset and ran home. After discussing what Harriet did to help Mrs. Hoozit, ask children where they might plant seeds if they did not have space for a garden. Discuss rooftop gardens, windowboxes, and other examples of gardens in small spaces.

Tell the children that they will have the chance to grow their own plants. Ask them what they think they will need. Discuss how plants get started and what they need to grow. Bring out the pots, jars, or cups and demonstrate how the children might decorate them. Encourage the children to think of their own designs. Have the children decorate the cups using crayons or marking pens. Rickrack or other trimming might be glued around the cups.

After the cups are decorated, have the children put a layer of pebbles in the bottom for drainage. Then have them place potting soil in the cups to within about one inch of the top. Have each child make a small

depression in the soil and drop in one or more seeds. (*Note*: You may want to use the seeds from an orange, grapefruit, or lemon; put them in warm water overnight before you plant them.) Pat the soil over the seeds and water them. Put the pots near a sunny window.

When the children are finished planting, discuss how they will need to care for their plants.

Followup

Cut the top off a pineapple, leaving some of the fruit with it. Put the top on a paper towel for several days. Then plant it in a dish of pebbles or sand, covering everything but the leaves. Water it well. Have the children note the progress of the plant as it matures.

Sabin, Louis (retold by). *JOHNNY APPLESEED*
Mahwah, N.J.: Troll Assoc., 1985
also, Eva Moore. Nashville, Tenn.: Ideals, 1988; paperback, New York:
Scholastic Book Services, (no date)
The legend of Johnny Appleseed, folk hero who traveled America during the frontier days and planted apple trees for future settlers.

Materials

- small paper sacks
- green and red construction paper
- glue or paste
- scissors

Before You Read

Tell the children that the early settlers in this country liked to tell the story of a man they called Johnny Appleseed who roamed the wilderness planting apple trees. Tell them he is credited with helping to spread the trees throughout the country. Explain briefly how legends arise and how they may have a variety of versions. Tell them you will read one version of the Johnny Appleseed legend.

After You Read

Review the story with the children. Discuss the various apple products and the way apples are cooked or prepared.

You may wish to assemble the apple tree described below ahead of time and show it to the children. Tell them that they will make small apple trees to remind them of Johnny Appleseed. Explain step by step how to make the tree.

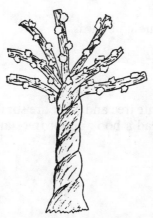

Steps

1. Cut the sack in straight strips from the opening to about half way down the sack.

2. Twist the half of the sack that is not cut to make the trunk of the tree.

3. Tear up small pieces of the green paper to make leaves for the tree. Paste them onto the branches.

4. Cut out small red circles for apples and paste them on the branches. You may want to use a large hole puncher to make the circles.

When the children have finished their trees, use the trees to decorate a seasonal bulletin board display.

Followup

You may also wish to read the following books to the children.

Udry, Janice May
A Tree Is Nice
New York: Harper & Row, 1956
The many uses of trees are described: for beauty, shade, and apples. A Caldecott award winner. Paint a large tree trunk on a sheet of paper. Use pieces of sponge dipped in paint to decorate the tree with leaves.

Carrick, Donald
The Tree
New York: Macmillan, 1971
Erik loves the tree in front of his house, but it becomes too large and is cut down. Through the seasons, Erik notices the loss of the tree, until a sapling is bought from a nursery and planted in its place. Make spatter-paint leaf designs or leaf etchings.

Udry, Janice May. *A TREE IS NICE*
New York: Harper & Row, 1956
Reasons why a tree is nice are mentioned in this book.

Materials

- leaves (oak leaves recommended)
- cloths, towels, carpet scraps for pounding boards
- stiff brushes or hair brushes

Before You Read

Ask the children if they have a favorite tree and what are some of the things that they like to do around trees. Tell them that you are going to read a book about trees and why trees are nice.

After You Read

Review the book by discussing the usefulness of trees, pointing out that trees are beautiful as well as useful. Tell the children that you will show them how to make leaf skeletons. Have the children put their leaves on a folded towel, cloth, or carpet scrap (any material that will yield to the pounding of the brush bristle). Next tell the children to pound the leaf with the brush (bristles down) for about five minutes or until the veins of the leaf show through. Tell them to pound evenly and carefully all over the leaf. Have the children look at each other's leaf patterns and compare them.

Followup

The children may want to preserve their leaves by ironing them between sheets of wax paper with a warm iron, or they may wish to begin making leaf collections.

Dr. Seuss. *McELLIGOT'S POOL*
New York: Random House, 1947
A farmer tells a boy all the reasons he will not catch fish in McElligot's pool,
but Marco thinks of all the places the pool might go and the kinds of fish he
might catch.

Materials

- colored tissue paper for fish shapes (see appendix A, page 128)
- facial tissues or toilet paper for stuffing
- paste or glue
- crayons
- scissors
- thread

Before You Read

Ask the children if they have ever been fishing or seen unusual fish in an aquarium. Tell the children that you will read a story about Marco and his wild imaginings about different kinds of fish.

After You Read

Ask the children what parts of the story were funny and if they thought some of the fish were unusual. Then tell them that they can make fish that are funny, strange, or unusual, too, because these fish will blow in the wind.

Distribute precut fish shapes, two to each child, or have the children cut out their own shapes. Be sure that they cut carefully through two sheets of tissue paper if they make their own shapes. Then explain step by step how to make the fish, but also encourage the children to use their imaginations in decorating the fish.

Steps

1. Draw a mouth, eyes, and a pattern of scales in one or more colors on one side of each tissue-paper fish piece.

2. Squeeze a thin line of glue along the inside edge of one piece of each fish, leaving the tail portion unglued.

3. Carefully press the unglued fish against the fish with glue to form a fishlike bag with the tail end open.

4. When the glue is dry, carefully fill the fish with tissue.

5. Make a small hole at the top of the fish and attach the thread. Hang the fish up in a drafty place.

Freeman, Don. *MOP TOP*
New York: Viking Press, 1955; with cassette, Live Oak Media, 1982
Mop Top was the nickname for a boy who did not want to have his hair cut.
His mother sent him to the barber, but he went elsewhere. He does get his
hair cut at last for his birthday party.

Materials

- solid-colored stockings (one per child)
- cotton batting for stuffing
- orange yarn
- large-eye needles
- heavy thread
- crayons or marking pens

Before You Read

Ask the children if any of them has recently had a haircut. Ask them if they enjoyed it or not and why. Tell them that you will read a story about a boy who did not like getting his hair cut and did everything he could to avoid it.

After You Read

Briefly review the story by discussing how different a person can look after his or her hair is cut or restyled. Ask the children if they have ever known anyone with hair like Mop Top's. Then tell them that they can make a doll with hair like Mop Top's. You may wish to assemble a doll according to the directions below ahead of time to show the children. (*Note*: It is best to do this activity in small groups of five children or fewer.) Explain step by step how to assemble the dolls.

Steps

1. Draw a face on one side of the toe of the sock.

2. Stuff the toe of the sock with cotton to make a round head.

3. Tie a string around the stuffed sock toe to make the head. Leave the string loose enough so that the child's finger will fit up into the head to move it.

4. Sew the orange yarn on the head of the puppet for hair. Do this by wrapping the yarn about five times around your fingers and cutting off that amount. Sew this yarn on the head using large in-and-out stitches.

5. The children may wish to color the bottom of the sock, sew buttons on for decoration, or tie a bow around the neck.

Followup

Have the children use their puppets to act out the story of Mop Top.

Munroe, Roxie. *CHRISTMASTIME IN NEW YORK*
New York: Dodd, Mead, 1987
This is a visual tour of New York City at Christmastime. Although there is no story, there is an annotated list of sights and brief history.

Materials

- aluminum foil
- popped corn and/or cranberries
- pine cones
- spools
- string, ribbon, thread, needles
- pipe cleaners
- sparkles, beads
- scissors
- glue

Before You Read

Ask the children how their town or city changes to get ready for Christmas. Then tell the children that you are going to look at a book about Christmas in New York City. Turn through the pages slowly, allowing them time to discuss the sights. Let the children comment upon how the sights are similar or different from their hometown or city.

After You Read

Tell the children that there are many kinds of materials available for making Christmas decorations. Show them the materials you have assembled. You may wish to complete the ornaments described below ahead of time to show the children. Tell them you will show them how to make a variety of ornaments.

Catherine Bach

Ornaments

- Crumple up aluminum foil to make silver balls. Put one end of a piece of string in the foil first to hang it by.

- String popcorn, cranberries, or both using a needle and thread.

- Poke pipe cleaners through thread spools and bend the wire at the bottom to prevent it from slipping out. Bend the cleaner at the other end to form a hook. Glue ribbon or sparkles to the spool.

- Wrap a pipe cleaner around a pine cone and form a hook for hanging. Glue beads, sparkles, bits of ribbon or foil to the cone.

Allow the children to create their own decorations. They may need help threading needles or tying string. You may wish to suggest that they make an ornament to give to someone as a gift.

Krasilovsky, Phyllis. *THE MAN WHO DIDN'T WASH HIS DISHES*
Garden City, N.Y.: Doubleday, 1950; paperback, 1978
A man living alone hates to wash his dishes. Each night he uses different
dishes until he has no clean ones left. At last a rainstorm helps get the
dishes clean.

Materials

- paper plates (one per child)
- crayons

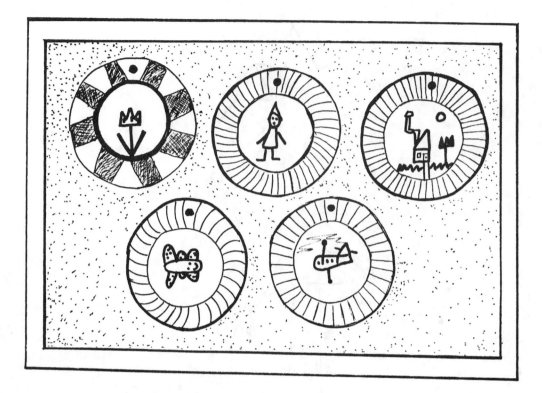

Before You Read

Ask the children if they ever help with chores around their home. Discuss whatever jobs they might do. Ask if any of them has ever washed dishes. Tell them you will read a story about a man who did not like to wash dishes.

After You Read

Tell the children that they will make a special dish of their own that they will not have to wash because it is meant to be hung on the wall. Pass out the paper plates and crayons to the children. Encourage them to think of their own pictures or designs to draw on the plates. Use the plates for a bulletin board display when the children are finished.

Brown, Marc. *ARTHUR'S CHRISTMAS*
Boston: Little, Brown, 1984
Arthur has problems trying to choose a gift for Santa Claus. Finally he decides
to watch Santa and see what foods he likes.

Materials

- cardboard stars (one per child)
- glitter
- glue
- crayons
- hole puncher
- string or ribbon

Before You Read

Ask the children if they have ever had trouble trying to choose a gift for someone. Tell them that in the story you will read, Arthur is trying to find the right gift for Santa.

After You Read

Review the story by asking the children why Arthur bought so many different foods, and who they think put the note on the Christmas tree. Suggest that a gift for someone might be something that they could make, such as a Christmas star. Tell them that you will show them how to make a star that they will be able to hang on a tree or in a window, or to give to a friend as a gift.

Distribute precut stars. Suggest ways the children might decorate them with crayons and glitter. When the children have finished decorating their stars, punch a hole in the top point of each star, place the ribbon or string through the hole, and tie it. Remind the children that they might give the stars as gifts.

Followup

Ask the children the next day what they decided to do with their stars.

Miles, Betty. *A HOUSE FOR EVERYONE*
New York: Alfred A. Knopf, 1958
People live in many different ways in many different types of homes.

Materials

- shoeboxes or other small boxes (one per child)
- wallpaper pieces or construction paper
- magazines
- playdough (optional)
- empty thread spools
- paste
- scissors
- crayons

Nick
Klinger

Before You Read

Ask the children how many different kinds of homes they know about, for example, an apartment, a teepee, an igloo, a houseboat. Suggest some of these if they cannot think of them. Then tell the children that you will read a book about different kinds of homes and different ways of living.

After You Read

Tell the children that they can make a small home of their own. Bring out the boxes and ask the children to think about how they could make the inside of the box look like the inside of a home with the roof removed. Discuss how a home looks on the inside. Point out that they may want to decorate the walls with paper or paste pictures cut from magazines onto the walls. After the children have developed some ideas about how they will decorate their homes, let them begin work. The spools and playdough may be used to make furniture for the house.

Followup

You may also wish to read the following book to the children.

Burton, Virginia Lee
The Little House
Boston: Houghton Mifflin, 1942, 1978
A little house located in the country is unhappy when the city grows up all around it. Through an unexpected turn of events, the little house finds itself in the country again and is happy once more.

Lionni, Leo. *LITTLE BLUE AND LITTLE YELLOW*
New York: Astor-Honor, 1959
A story about the colors blue and yellow who, when they hug each other, turn
green, until their parents make them separate.

Materials

- blue, red, and yellow tempera paint
- pie pans
- sponge pieces cut in shapes
- drawing paper

Before You Read

Play a game with the children in which you select a colored object in the room, blue for example, and make a statement such as, "I see something blue." Ask the children to guess the object you are thinking of. Then the children may want to take turns selecting objects and guessing what they are. Next tell the children that you will read them a book about two colors, blue and yellow.

After You Read

Tell the children that they will have the chance to experiment with colors. Have them put on their paint shirts. Put each color of tempera paint into a separate pan and place the collection of sponge shapes nearby. Tell the children to dip the pieces of sponge in the paints and then press them lightly on their sheets of drawing paper. Encourage them to make original designs and to experiment with the colors. Point out that where the colors overlap, new colors will be created. When the children are finished, discuss their paintings and use them in a bulletin board display.

Followup

You may also wish to read the following book to the children.

Lobel, Arnold
The Great Blueness and Other Predicaments
New York: Harper & Row, 1968
The Great Greyness was a time when there were no colors in the world. A wizard tries to improve things by coloring the world first blue, then yellow, and finally red. No one is happy, however, until he hits on the idea of mixing colors and using them all.

Kellogg, Steven. ISLAND OF THE SKOG
New York: Dial Press, 1973; paperback, 1976
The mice are finding life dangerous, and decide to sail away to a safer place. They journey to the Island of the Skog where, fearing the unknown Skog, they bombard the land with cannonballs before setting foot upon it.

Materials

- plastic foam packing pieces
- glue
- toothpicks
- watercolors

Before You Read

Ask the children if they have ever heard of an animal called a skog. Tell them that the mice in the story that you are about to read had never heard of or seen a skog either, so they were afraid of it.

After You Read

Review the story by asking the children why the skog pretended to be a big monster and why the mice fired cannonballs at the land. Ask the children if they noticed where the cannonballs landed. Discuss the kinds of things that make people frightened, particularly the unknown or not knowing.

Next, tell the children that they can create their own new animals. You may want to assemble a foam animal ahead of time to show to the children. Demonstrate how to make the animals by gluing or sticking together the plastic foam pieces using toothpicks or glue. Point out that faces and colors can be painted on when the animals are completed. (*Note*: You may need to add glue or liquid soap to the paint to make it adhere to some types of plastic foam.)

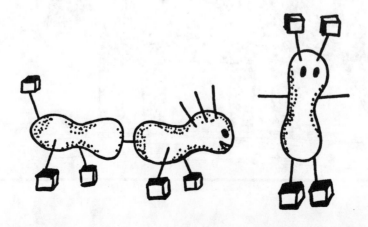

When the animals are completed, the children may wish to assemble them on a display table and call it a classroom zoo of new animals. Encourage the children to name their animals and explain why the name is appropriate or what the animal can do that makes it special.

Yolen, Jane. *OWL MOON*
New York: Putnam, 1987
A little girl and her father go out on a snowy wintery night looking for an owl.
A Caldecott award winner.

Materials

- blue and white construction paper
- glue or paste

Before You Read

Ask the children to think about the kinds of things they can do in the winter. Tell them you will read a story about a special kind of walk that a little girl and her father take on a snowy winter night.

After You Read

Ask the children if they have ever seen or heard an owl on a winter's night. Explain why they would have to look for an owl at night. Talk about the sounds the owl makes. Point out to the children that sometimes it is fun to be inside where it is warm and make pictures of outdoor fun. Show them a partially completed picture that you have made using blue construction paper and torn bits of white paper. Show the children how to make pictures and designs using the torn paper and pasting it on the blue background. (An alternative to using the torn white paper is to use white rice.)

Ask the children to think of a winter activity and then make a picture of it. Later, you may wish to have the children dictate stories about their pictures or make a winter bulletin-board display.

Tresselt, Alvin (retold by). *THE MITTEN*
New York: Lothrop, Lee & Shepard, 1964; paperback, Scholastic Book
Services, 1985
An old folktale about a boy who loses a mitten in the snow. Many animals come along and make a home in it to be warm until the mitten bursts open. The boy returns to find his mitten very worn and does not know why.

Materials

- colored construction paper
- crayons
- yarn

Before You Read

Tell the children that you will read a folktale. Briefly explain that folktales are stories that are sometimes based on facts and sometimes are just made up for fun or to teach a lesson.

After You Read

Ask the children if they think what happened in the story could have been true. Ask them if there was anything in the story that seemed unreal. Why? Next tell the children that you will show them how to make their own make-believe mittens. You may wish to assemble a pair of mittens according to the directions below ahead of time.

Steps

1. Demonstrate to the children how to fold a sheet of construction paper in half across the width.

2. Tell them to watch as you place your hand down flat on the paper and trace loosely around the fingers to form the outline of a mitten.

3. Show the children how to carefully hold the two sides of the paper together as you cut out the mittens.

4. Then tell them to decorate the mittens using the crayons.

5. Punch holes at the top of the mittens and draw a piece of yarn through the holes.

The yarn can then be tied and used to hang the mittens. The completed mittens can be used to make a bulletin board display or taken home.

Followup

Recite for the children the nursery rhyme about the three little kittens who lost their mittens.

Teacher Resources: Art, Holidays

Adler, David A. *HANUKKAH FUNBOOK: PUZZLES, RIDDLES, MAGIC & MORE*
Brooklyn, N.Y.: Hebrew Publ., 1976; paperback, 1978
Activities for Hanukkah.
holidays

Adler, David A. *A PICTURE BOOK OF HANUKKAH*
New York: Holiday, 1982; paperback, 1985
Information about Hanukkah.
holidays

Bulla, Clyde Robert. *SAINT VALENTINE'S DAY*
New York: Thomas Y. Crowell, 1965
The story of St. Valentine's Day and how it is celebrated today. Describes how to make various cards.
holiday art

Cole, Ann; Haas, Carolyn; Bushnell, Faith; and Betty Weinberger. *I SAW A PURPLE COW AND 100 OTHER RECIPES FOR LEARNING*
Boston: Little, Brown, 1972
Arts and crafts ideas for early childhood.
art

Cole, Ann; Haas, Carolyn; Bushnell, Faith; and Betty Weinberger. *A PUMPKIN IN A PEAR TREE: CREATIVE IDEAS FOR TWELVE MONTHS OF HOLIDAY FUN*
Boston: Little, Brown, 1976
Appropriate ideas for grades 1 through 6.
art

Flemming, Bonnie Mack; Hamilton, Darlene Softley; and JoAnne Deal Hicks. *RESOURCES FOR CREATIVE TEACHING IN EARLY CHILDHOOD EDUCATION*
New York: Harcourt Brace Jovanovich, 1977
Holiday art including New Year's, Halloween, Thanksgiving, Christmas, and Hanukkah. Bibliography.
holiday art

Gaitskell, Charles, and Al Hurwitz. *CHILDREN AND THEIR ART: METHODS FOR THE ELEMENTARY SCHOOL*, 4th ed.
New York: Harcourt Brace Jovanovich, 1982
Includes analysis of the slow learner and gifted child. Textbook.
art

Guilfoile, Elizabeth. *VALENTINE'S DAY*
Champaign, Ill.: Garrard, 1965
Origins of St. Valentine's Day and how it is celebrated.
holidays

Herberholz, Barbara. *EARLY CHILDHOOD ART*, 3d ed.
Dubuque, Iowa: William C. Brown, 1985

Lowenfeld, Viktor, and W. Lambert Brittan. *CREATIVE AND MENTAL GROWTH*, 7th ed.
New York: Macmillan, 1982
Development of artistic expression in children ages two through twelve. Also classroom procedures and the relationship between teacher and pupil. Textbook.
art

Perl, Lila, and Alma F. Ada. *PINATAS & PAPER FLOWERS—PINATAS Y FLORES DE PAPEL: HOLIDAYS OF THE AMERICAS IN ENGLISH & SPANISH*
Burlington, Maine: Houghton-Mifflin, 1983
art

Simon, Norma. *HANUKKAH*
New York: Thomas Y. Crowell, 1966
Details of the holiday and its origins.
holidays

Children's Books: Art, Holidays

Aleichem, Sholem. *HANUKKAH MONEY*
New York: Greenwillow Books, 1978
A humorous story about Hanukkah celebration with a Russian setting. Describes the foreign money and its equivalents.
Hanukkah game

Amoss, Bertha. *WHAT DID YOU LOSE SANTA?*
New York: Harper & Row, 1987
Santa and Mrs. Claus look everywhere in this textless picture book to find the banner that Santa lost. It says "Peace on Earth" and trails behind the sleigh.
Christmas pictures

Balian, Lorna. *SOMETIMES IT'S TURKEYS SOMETIMES IT'S FEATHERS*
Nashville, Tenn.: Abingdon Press, 1973
Old Mrs. Gumm finds a turkey egg and raises the bird for Thanksgiving dinner. On the big day, she tries to kill the turkey but cannot. Stuffed paper bag turkey or hand-outline turkey.

Calhoun, Mary. *WOBBLE THE WITCH CAT*
New York: William Morrow, 1958
Wobble is afraid to ride on a broomstick but finds a vacuum cleaner more to its liking. Witch cat pictures with precut black paper circles and ovals, and pasted-on or drawn features.

Duvoisin, Roger. *EASTER TREAT*
New York: Alfred A. Knopf, 1954
Santa Claus goes south in disguise to have an Easter vacation. Fingerprint paint spring flowers.

Ets, Marie Hall, and Aurora Labastida. *NINE DAYS TO CHRISTMAS: A STORY OF MEXICO*
New York: E. P. Dutton, 1978
Ceci, a Mexican child, looks forward to Christmas and its traditional celebration, including the breaking of the pinata. A Caldecott award winner.
Pinata

Frost, Robert. *STOPPING BY WOODS ON A SNOWY EVENING*
New York: E. P. Dutton, 1978
A picture book illustrating the well-known poem. Snow pictures: white chalk on blue construction paper, or white spatter-paint on blue paper with pin-down patterns.

Lindgren, Astrid. *CHRISTMAS IN THE STABLE*
New York: Coward, McCann & Geoghegan, 1962; paperback, Putnam, 1979
Picture book of the Christmas story. *Christmas is* book: each child draws a picture on a spirit master of what Christmas means to him or her; the teacher adds a sentence dictated by the child; copies of all the pictures go into a class book.

Lionni, Leo. *FREDERICK*
New York: Pantheon Books, 1966
All of the mice get ready for winter in the traditional ways except Frederick, who says he is gathering words and colors. Later when the mice become bored, Frederick recites colorful stories and poetry about the four seasons. Winter scenes painted with sponge pieces.

Minarik, Else Holmelund. *LITTLE BEAR*
New York: Harper & Row, 1957; cassette, 1986
Seasonal stories centering around Mother Bear and Little Bear. Glue coffee grounds in bear-head outline to construction paper; color in facial features.

Moore, Clement C. *THE NIGHT BEFORE CHRISTMAS*
Racine, Wis.: Western, 1985
The traditional story of the visit of St. Nicholas. Other editions: Grosset & Dunlap, 1961; Random House, 1975; Doubleday, 1977; paperback, Ideals, 1975. Santa-head decoration from paper plate, cotton, and red construction paper; or, gift box pictures: draw a gift box and glue on a picture of what is in it.

Provensen, Alice, and Martin Provensen. *A BOOK OF SEASONS*
New York: Random House, 1975; paperback, 1978
Things children do throughout the four seasons of the year. Fall: vegetable prints using okra, green pepper, or onion pieces dipped in paint.

Tresselt, Alvin. *HIDE AND SEEK FOG*
New York: Lothrop, Lee & Shepard, 1965
Things children do in the summer at the seashore when it is foggy. Blow-paint pictures using straws and tempera paint; or, watercolor paint on newsprint for blurred, foggy look.

Zolotow, Charlotte. *HOLD MY HAND*
New York: Harper & Row, 1972
Two friends play together in the winter. Snowflakes cut from thin, white folded paper.

COOKING

Learning through Cooking

Children of all ages enjoy preparing and cooking food. For young children, such activities can aid language development as well as provide opportunities for learning new skills and concepts. Food preparation tasks can help teach sequencing, counting, measuring, and following directions at the same time the children are having fun. Concepts of nutrition, health, science, and safety are also easily related to cooking activities.

Cooking and food preparation experiences give children real motivation to practice prereading skills without conscious awareness or prompting. Children learn to follow a printed line from left to right and to move down a recipe chart. Illustrations in charts encourage children to predict the content of a direction. Through group reading and discussion of the ingredient and direction charts, children improve their language skills.

Food in Literature

There are a number of books written for young children in which food plays a major part. Books like Tomie DePaola's *Pancakes for Breakfast* (Harcourt Brace Jovanovich, 1978) naturally motivate children to make the foods in the stories. In other stories, such as Beatrix Potter's *Peter Rabbit* (Putnam, 1981; Ideals, 1986), food is not an element of the plot, but the story can still stimulate interest in food preparation—for example, making a rabbit-shaped cake or carrot cake or salad.

Description

Cooking and food preparation may range from simple beginning activities such as making butter, in which no cutting, measuring, or cooking is involved, to complicated activities such as baking gingerbread men.

A few cooking utensils and a source of heat for cooking are essential for most preparations. The heat source may be a hot plate, electric fry pan, oven, stove, or microwave. It is also advisable to have a means of keeping foods cool such as a refrigerator or ice chest.

Before using any recipe, it is a good practice for you to pretest the recipe, assemble supplies and equipment, and make safety arrangements. It is usually a good idea to make up simple recipe charts that list the ingredients and directions for preparing the food. If the activity can be done with a large group, you may want to use charts the size of poster boards with approximately 2-inch-high lettering. For activities involving one to four children, a smaller tabletop stand-up recipe book might be used. Recipe charts for some of the activities in this chapter appear in the appendix.

Since cooking experiences are guided by the teacher, they are usually best performed with a small group of children (six or fewer) so that everyone has a chance to participate and watch. If the tasks involve the use of knives, peeling, or using a heat source, then only two children should be working on that job and should be under direct adult supervision.

It is important to stress good health habits and safety when preparing food. Before beginning any food preparation, have the children involved wash their hands. Have the other children in the classroom settled at other activities that will not require your direct supervision or distract you from the cooking group.

Some food activities may be easily performed by the entire class. Examples are shelling peanuts for making peanut butter, making popcorn in an electric see-through popper, making butter in small baby food jars, or scooping out a classroom pumpkin. These large-group experiences may involve aspects of smelling, tasting, feeling, and doing, but not the use of sharp tools. For some activities, it is best to have a small group make up the dough or batter, and then let the whole class cut out cookies or decorate the food product. For other food activities, you will want to have one small group prepare the food for the whole class. If this is done, assure the other children that they, too, will have their turn at cooking.

If a small group prepares the food, you may wish to have your cooks for that day explain to the class what they used (the ingredients) and how they prepared the food (the directions). In this way, the children receive further practice in recall and memory skills, sequencing, and language use.

Prior to reading a story that will motivate cooking, have your charts and supplies prepared. Have a plan for the physical arrangements and activities clearly developed. After reading the story, assemble your group for the cooking activity. You may wish to follow the procedure below.

1. Read the title of the recipe to the children while pointing to the words on the chart.

2. Ask the children to "read" the title of the recipe with you. Point to the words as you all say them together.

3. Read each item on the ingredients chart. As you read each item, point to the words on the chart. Ask the children to repeat the words.

4. After you have read the entire list of ingredients, you might review it by asking the children what item is needed first, second, and so on.

5. Read the directions chart one step at a time. Again, have the children repeat the directions step by step with you.

6. When you have read the two charts, begin working with the ingredients. Be sure the children wash their hands. Ask the children to tell you the first ingredient. Have a child measure out the amount needed, reread the directions, and follow them.

7. Give all the children involved a chance to help in the preparation.

8. As you are working with the children, talk about where the ingredients come from, how they smell or taste, and their color or texture.

9. Have the group or class share in eating the finished product.

Overview

The books and recipes in this chapter are only a sample of those that young children would enjoy. A list of additional children's books that lend themselves to cooking activities is included at the end of this chapter, as well as a brief list of resource books for your use. Keep in mind, too, that many poems and nursery rhymes mention food and can be used to stimulate cooking activities.

Activities

Aliki. *CORN IS MAIZE: THE GIFT OF THE INDIANS*
New York: Thomas Y. Crowell, 1976
Simple explanations of how corn grows, how it was first cultivated, how the Indians used it, how it was introduced to the Pilgrims, and how it is important in the world today. Nonfiction. Back of the book: how to make a corn husk wreath.

Materials

- recipe chart for popcorn (see appendix B, page 129)
- ingredients: popcorn, cooking oil, butter or margarine, salt
- large pan with cover, or electric popcorn maker
- large bowl
- dried ears of corn (optional)

Before You Read

Ask the children to name a few of the ways we prepare corn to eat. Then tell them that you will read a book that explains the history of corn, how it grows, and how we use it. (*Note*: You may want to read only a part of the book at one time.)

After You Read

Briefly review the important details of what you have read. Then tell the children that they can make popcorn. Assemble the ingredients and necessary accessories. Help the children read the recipe chart (see the suggestions at the beginning of this chapter). When the popcorn is ready, serve it to the class on napkins.

You might wish to show dried corn or colorful Indian corn to the children.

Cosgrove, Stephen. *THE MUFFIN MUNCHER*
Los Angeles, Calif.: Price, Stern, Sloan, 1974, 1975; Mankato, Minn.: Creative Education, 1978
A dragon enters a kingdom whose economy is based on making muffins. When the dragon, who loves muffins, eats up all that are produced, the people become poor. The solution is that the dragon agrees to fire the ovens in return for a share of the muffins.

Materials

- muffin mix
- muffin pans
- flat-bottomed ice cream cones
- mixing bowl, measuring cup, mixing spoons

Before You Read

Ask the children if they have heard of dragons. Ask them to describe what they think a dragon would look like and how it would act. Point out that some dinosaurs resembled what dragons might look like if they were real. Tell the children that you will read a story about a dragon that was unusual because it liked to eat muffins. Before you begin, be sure the children understand the meaning of the word *munch*.

Josh Beers

After You Read

Ask the children to tell you what it was that the dragon liked to eat. Then ask the children if they have ever made muffins. Tell the children that some of them will make muffins for the class. Select four or five children to make the muffins.

Have enough muffin mix on hand to make a muffin for each child. Read the directions on the muffin mix package to the children. It is usually necessary only to add water and/or eggs to the mix. When the batter is mixed and ready, have the children fill the ice cream cones about two-thirds full with the batter and place the cones in the muffin pan cups for baking. Put the muffins in the oven to bake yourself.

Have the children clean the utensils while they are waiting for the muffins to bake. The muffin dough will rise in the cones to form a rounded top like a scoop of ice cream. When they are done, allow them to cool briefly, then serve.

Followup

A small group of children may want to act out the story. One child may play the dragon, one the king, and several others the bakers. Get the children started by retelling the story as the children pantomime their roles. Later the children can begin speaking their parts.

Devlin, Wende, and Harry Devlin. *CRANBERRY THANKSGIVING*
New York: Parents' Magazine Press, 1971; reprint, 1980
Maggie's grandmother invites dapper Mr. Horace to Thanksgiving dinner.
Maggie asks her friend, shabby, colorful Mr. Whiskers to join them. When
one of the two guests tries to steal an old recipe for cranberry bread, grand-
mother learns a lesson about human nature: "clothes don't make the man."

Materials

- ingredients for Grandmother's Famous Cranberry Bread (see back of book)
- mixing bowl, mixing spoons
- loaf pan

Before You Read

Ask the children if there is something special they like to eat for Thanksgiving dinner. Tell them that
you will read a story about a Thanksgiving dinner during which a problem occurs.

After You Read

Ask the children why they think Mr. Horace took the recipe for cranberry bread. Who helped get the
recipe back? What did Grandmother learn about Mr. Horace? How did she feel about Mr. Whiskers then?

Tell the children that they can make some of Grandmother's Famous Cranberry Bread. Select a small
group of cooks and let them prepare the bread with your guidance. Follow the recipe on the back cover of
the book.

Adams, Adrienne. *A WOGGLE OF WITCHES*
New York: Charles Scribner's Sons, 1971
This is a humorous account of how a woggle (group) of witches lives and feasts
in the forest.

Materials

- recipe chart for Peanut Butter Yummies (see appendix B, page 129)
- ingredients: ⅔ cup peanut butter, ½ cup corn syrup, 1½ cups graham cracker crumbs, 1 cup nonfat dry milk, ½ cup powdered sugar
- mixing bowl, mixing spoon, measuring cup
- rolling pin
- waxed paper

Before You Read

Ask the children what kinds of things they think about at Halloween. Prompt them, if necessary, by
mentioning black cats, witches, costumes, trick-or-treat, and goblins. Tell the children that you are going to
read a story about how a woggle of witches spends its night.

After You Read

Talk about the things that the witches did in the forests. One of those activities was to feast or eat, just
as children might do at a Halloween party.

Tell the children that they will make a special treat that might be served at a Halloween party. Select five or six children to prepare the Peanut Butter Yummies. Help the children read the recipe chart (see the suggestions at the beginning of this chapter). Help the children measure and mix the ingredients according to the recipe. Serve the Peanut Butter Yummies to the class.

Followup

Witch cats can easily be made by young children if you provide them with precut black paper circles and larger ovals. The circle serves as the head and is glued to the oval, which is the body. The children can then cut or tear pieces of black paper to make the ears and tail of the cat. Other features may be drawn on the cat using chalk or white crayon.

Foreman, Michael. *WAR AND PEAS*
New York: Thomas Y. Crowell, 1974
King Lion, his country faced with a severe drought, goes off for help from a
nearby country where there is plenty of food. However, Fat King refuses to
help and chases King Lion back to his land where a battle ensues. As a result,
the ground is dug up and when rain comes there is food for all.

Materials

- recipe chart for Royal Sandwiches (see appendix B, page 130)
- ingredients: softened cream cheese, small jar of pimientos, green pepper, pitted black olives, bread slices
- knife
- cookie cutters, or jars and glasses of various sizes to cut out different shapes from bread slices

Before You Read

Tell the children that you will read a story about two kingdoms, one in which there was not enough
food and one in which there was more than enough.

After You Read

Briefly review the story by asking the children how overeating affected the Fat King and the people of
his country. Discuss the idea that overeating is unhealthy for animals and humans. Then tell the children
that they can make Royal Sandwiches, fit for a king. Help the children read the recipe chart (see the suggestions at the beginning of this chapter). Also help them in cutting the ingredients, or cut a variety of shapes
yourself and let the children choose them to construct their sandwiches. Encourage the children to create
original designs on their sandwiches. When the children are finished making their sandwiches, you may wish
to display the sandwiches on a platter before the children eat them.

Galdone, Paul. *THE GINGERBREAD BOY*
New York: Houghton Mifflin, 1975; paperback, 1983
**Also Cutts, David. Mahwah, N.J.: Troll, 1979; New York: paperback, Mac-
millan, 1988; Wilburn, Kathy. New York: Putnam, 1984; McGill-Franzen,
Anne. Milwaukee, Wis. Raintree, 1979**
An old couple want to have a son so badly that a gingerbread boy springs to
life. The cookie has a restless spirit, however, and runs away from the couple,
a cow, a horse, threshers and mowers, but finally is outwitted by a clever fox.

Materials

- recipe chart for gingerbread cookie dough (optional, see appendix B, page 130)
- ingredients: 4 cups sifted flour, 1 teaspoon baking soda, 1 tablespoon powdered ginger, ¼ teaspoon salt, 1 cup margarine, ½ cup brown sugar, ¾ cup molasses, 2 eggs, raisins
- mixing bowls, spoons, measuring cup and spoons
- cookie sheets, aluminum foil
- spatula

Before You Read

Ask the children if they have ever heard the story of the Gingerbread Boy. Tell them it is an old story
about a boy made of gingerbread who comes alive and gets into trouble when he runs away from his home.

After You Read

Briefly review the story by asking the children to recount the adventure of the Gingerbread Boy. Then tell them that they can make their own gingerbread boys. For very young children, have the dough already made up and let the children form their own gingerbread boys. For upper primary children, prepare a recipe chart (see appendix B, page 130) and have the children prepare the dough with your guidance. A group of four or five children is best to prepare the dough.

When the dough is mixed and ready, give each child a small ball of dough about 1½ inches in diameter and a piece of aluminum foil. Have the children flour their foil to prevent the dough from sticking and then arrange their dough into a gingerbread boy. If some children have trouble forming the shape of the body, suggest that they make only the face by flattening the dough into a circle. Once the dough is formed into a cookie, the children can decorate it with the raisins. When the cookie is decorated, use a permanent marker pen to write the child's name or initials on the foil. Place the cookies on baking sheets and cook until lightly brown, about 8 to 12 minutes. Allow the cookies to cool briefly before serving.

Followup

Make a set of flannelboard characters for the story and use them to tell the story. Then let the children retell the story using the flannelboard characters. Help them show events in the correct sequence and recall the refrain.

Christmas tree ornaments in the shape of gingerbread boys can be made from salt-flour dough using cookie cutters. They can be decorated with paint and sparkles. The recipe for salt-flour dough follows.

- ingredients: 1 cup salt, 2 cups flour, 1 cup water
- directions: mix ingredients together and roll out to approximately ¼-inch thick, cut or create ornaments, bake at 325° F for about 30 minutes, cool and decorate

Cooper, Susan (retold by). *SILVER COW: A WELSH TALE*
New York: Atheneum, 1983
High up in the hills of Wales, a young boy plays a harp which brings a silver cow
from the lake. The cow produces so much milk that the family becomes rich.
However, when the cow is old and can no longer give milk, the father decides
to butcher the cow and learns the price of greed.

Materials

- 1 or 2 cups of heavy cream
- small baby food jars with lids (one per child) or two plastic glasses with snap-on lids and two marbles
- crackers
- tablespoon, plastic knife
- salt in shaker

Before You Read

Ask the children if they know what animal helps us make butter. Briefly discuss cows as a source of
milk and milk products such as cream, butter, and cheese. Then tell the children that you are going to read a
story from long ago called a folktale, because people told it to children, who grew up and told it to their
children, and so the story was passed along by folks. Tell the children that this story is about a cow, a very
special silver cow.

After You Read

Briefly review the story by asking the children if they thought the father should kill the cow and why or
why not. Ask how the silver cow was different from cows they have known, and how it was the same.
Discuss the products of cow's milk and tell the children that you have cream from which butter is made.
Explain that butter is made from cream by shaking the cream until it forms butter.

All the children in the class can easily participate in this activity. If you use baby food jars, measure out
two tablespoons of cream into each jar. Close the lid tightly and have each child shake his or her own jar of
cream. The jar must be well shaken for about 10 minutes to form the butter. You may need to assist young
children in shaking the jars sufficiently.

If you use plastic cups, pour ½ cup of cream into each cup and add a large clean marble. The marble
will help agitate the cream and form the butter faster. Secure the tops and pass the cups to be shaken 10
hard shakes by each child around a circle of class members. As they shake the cups the children may enjoy
repeating:

> Shaking, shaking, the cream from the cow,
> Change the cream into butter now.

Occasionally stop and check the progress of the butter. Point out to the children the gradual change from a
liquid cream to solid particles of butter and milky water.

When the butter is ready, pass out napkins, crackers, and plastic knives. Remove the marbles if they
were used. Let the children spread the butter on the crackers and taste it. Ask the children if they think it
tastes different from butter bought in a store. Explain that the butter they buy probably has been chilled
and had salt added. They may wish to sprinkle a little salt on their butter.

Talk about the color of the butter. What color was the cream? What color is the butter? How has the
cream changed?

Followup

Draw or cut out pictures of the food products made from milk.

Ice cream can be easily made in the classroom, but the activity takes about 30 minutes. Refer to the following book for instructions.

Wilms, Barbara
Crunchy Bananas and Other Great Recipes Kids Can Cook
Layton, Utah: Sagamore Books, 1975; paperback, Falcon, 1984

McMillan, Bruce. *APPLES, HOW THEY GROW*
Boston: Houghton Mifflin, 1979
This book uses photographs and simplified text to describe how apples grow from buds to fruit. It also has a slightly more detailed explanation which an adult might use for background information. A glossary of terms is included at the end of the book.

Materials

- apples (one half per child)
- small marshmallows
- box of raisins
- box of toothpicks
- waxed paper

Before You Read

Tell the children that you will read a book that uses photographs to explain how apples grow.

After You Read

Briefly review the events in the development of apples by asking the children to recall them while looking at the photographs. Next discuss the different ways in which we eat apples. Then tell the children that today they will get a chance to make funny-face apples.

Give each child a half of an apple on a piece of waxed paper. Tell the children to use the marshmallows, raisins, and toothpicks to design funny-face apples.

When the children have finished, let them show their apples to the rest of the class before eating them. Be sure the children remove the toothpicks before eating the apples.

Followup

Play a game called "Who's got the apple?" Using a plastic apple, have one child hide it while the other children cover their eyes. Tell the children that the apple must be hidden so that it can be seen; it must not be inside anything or require anything to be moved or touched to find it. When the apple is hidden, the others in the class try to find it.

Whoever sees the apple first returns to his or her place and says, "I found the apple." Give the other children a few minutes to try to find the apple, too. You may want to give them clues. When most of the children have spotted the apple, have the child who found it first hide it again.

McCloskey, Robert. *BLUEBERRIES FOR SAL*
New York: Viking Press, 1948
Sal and her mother go on a blueberry picking trip. Sal wanders off and meets
a mother bear and her cub.

Materials

- fresh or frozen blueberries (about 2 pints)
- sugar (optional)
- milk (optional)
- serving bowls and spoons
- sieve

Before You Read

Ask the children if they have ever picked or tasted blueberries. Ask them if they know how blueberries
grow. Tell them you will read a story about a girl and her mother who go picking blueberries.

After You Read

Briefly discuss the sequence of events in the story. Then tell the children that they can taste blueberries
for themselves. Explain how blueberries are prepared. First, wash them in a sieve. Next, place the berries in
individual cups for each child. Serve the berries. The children may also want to taste the berries with sugar
and milk.

Discuss the flavor and color of the berries. Point out that the color in the berries could be used to paint
a picture or make food coloring. Have the children look in a mirror at their tongues after eating the berries.
What do they see?

Orbach, Ruth. *APPLE PIGS*
Cleveland, Ohio: William Collins & World, 1976; paperback, New York:
Putnam, 1981
A family, suddenly inundated with apples from a once dried-up tree, finds
enjoyable ways to use up the huge surplus crop. One solution is to make "apple
pigs," which are described at the end of the book.

Materials

- recipe chart for uncooked applesauce (optional, see appendix B, page 131)
- ingredients: (for 8 servings) 4 apples, ¼ cup water, ¼ cup sugar, 1 teaspoon cinnamon
- blender
- measuring cup, teaspoon
- knives

Before You Read

Ask the children to name several different ways they have eaten apples, for example, raw or in a pie.
Tell them that you will read a book about a family who had a lot of apples and wanted to find different
ways to use them.

After You Read

Briefly discuss the various ways the family in the story found to use apples. Then tell the children that they can make something from apples, too—applesauce.

For very young children, have the apples already peeled and halved. You may allow them to cut the apples into chunks or you may want to do this yourself. Older children can peel and core the apples and cut them into chunks. See appendix B, page 131, if you want to use a recipe chart.

When the apples have been washed, cored, peeled, and cut into chunks, the blending process can begin. Have the children measure the water and pour it into the blender. Next add the apple pieces. Add the sugar and cinnamon. Replace blender lid. Turn on the blender and watch the apples change into applesauce. Blending will take only a few seconds. Do not let the children get their fingers near the blender blades.

When the applesauce is ready, the children may want to spread it on graham crackers.

Followup

Have the children make apple pigs following the recipe at the end of *Apple Pigs*.

Apples may also be baked. Wash and core the apples and put them in a baking pan that has been rubbed with butter. Put 2 teaspoons of sugar and a piece of margarine in the core hole of each apple. Sprinkle with cinnamon. Add enough water to the pan so that it is about ½-inch deep. Cover the pan and bake at 350° F until the apples are soft (about 30 minutes). Serve hot or cold.

You may also wish to read the following book to the children.

Scheer, Julian.
Rain Makes Applesauce
New York: Holiday, 1964
Humorous story with the refrain: "and rain makes applesauce."

Make hot applesauce or applesauce-and-graham-cracker sandwiches.

Brooke

Ets, Marie Hall, and Aurora Labastida. *NINE DAYS TO CHRISTMAS*
New York: Viking Press, 1959
Ceci, a little Mexican girl, is excited about the plans being made for Christmas parties. Mexican customs and Spanish words are included in the story.

Materials

- a package of taco chips or taco shells
- sliced cheddar or American cheese (¼ lb.)
- a can of refried beans (enough for about 24 nachos)
- baking sheet
- plastic knives, spoon
- access to an oven, toaster oven, or microwave

Before You Read

Tell the children that you will read a story about a little Mexican girl, Ceci, who is waiting for Christmas to come.

After You Read

Briefly discuss the Mexican customs described in the story. Ask the children if they have ever been to a posada or seen a piñata. Then tell the children that they can make a snack similar to what Mexican-American children might enjoy in their homes.

Give each child a taco chip (or ¼ of a taco shell) and a plastic knife. Place a dish of refried beans nearby and have each child spread about a teaspoonful of beans on the chip. Next have each child place a small slice of cheese over the beans. The nachos are then ready to be placed on the baking sheet for heating.

Heat the nachos by placing them briefly under an oven broiler or in a toaster oven or microwave until the cheese melts. Serve warm.

Followup

You may wish to make a piñata designed from a box and covered with tissue paper and hang it in your classroom. You might also want to read the following book to the children.

Politi, Leo.
Song of the Swallows
New York: Charles Scribner's Sons, 1949
This takes place in Capistrano, California, where Juan, a Mexican boy, wonders about the return of the swallows on St. Joseph's Day. There are two songs with music in the book.

Rey, H. A. *CURIOUS GEORGE GETS A MEDAL*
Boston: Houghton Mifflin, 1957, 1974
Curious George, a monkey with a great deal of curiosity, becomes the first monkey in space.

Materials
- recipe chart for Monkey Sandwiches (see appendix B, page 131)
- ingredients: peanut butter, bananas (one half per child), raisins
- two slicing knives, plastic knives

Before You Read

Point out the word *curious* in the title and ask the children if they know what it means. Briefly discuss the meaning. Then tell them you will read a story about a very curious monkey.

After You Read

Ask the children to tell you what things happened to Curious George as a result of his curiosity. Ask them if they have ever gotten into strange or funny situations because of their curiosity.

Ask the children if they know what monkeys like to eat. If they do not mention it, point out that monkeys like fruit, and, in particular, bananas. Tell the children that they will make Monkey Sandwiches. Ask them to guess what the sandwiches will be made of.

Amanda Watkins

You may want to work with one-third or one-half of the class at a time. Help the children read the recipe chart (see the suggestions at the beginning of this chapter). When all the children have finished making sandwiches, have a Monkey Sandwich Party.

Followup

You may also want to read other Curious George books to the children. These include *Curious George Takes a Job*, *Curious George Rides a Bike*, *Curious George Flies a Kite*, and *Curious George Learns the Alphabet* (Houghton Mifflin).

Sendak, Maurice. *CHICKEN SOUP WITH RICE: A BOOK OF MONTHS*
New York: Harper & Row; cassette and paperback, 1986; Scholastic Book
Services, 1970
A short story in poetic form about eating chicken soup with rice any month of the year.

Materials

- chicken soup with rice (2 cans serve 10 children)
- water
- saucepan
- serving cups and spoons (one each per child)
- wooden spoon

Before You Read

Ask the children what kinds of soup they like to eat. Point out that many people believe that chicken soup is particularly good for someone with a cold. Tell them that you will read a story about how chicken soup with rice can be enjoyed at many different times.

After You Read

Have two or three children prepare the soup. You will need to open the cans, but the children can pour the soup into the pan and add water according to directions. Have the children stir the soup. Then put the soup on the stove to heat. When the soup is heated, measure it out into the children's cups.

Tresselt, Alvin. *WHITE SNOW, BRIGHT SNOW*
New York: Lothrop, Lee & Shepard, 1947
What people do when it snows. Poetic text evokes the atmosphere of a first snowfall. A Caldecott award winner.

Materials

- white cake mix
- butter frosting recipe chart (see appendix B, page 132)
- butter frosting ingredients: ½ cup margarine or butter, 2 cups powdered sugar, 1 teaspoon vanilla extract, 3 tablespoons milk, pinch of salt
- small candies for decorating
- muffin tins
- plastic knives, paper plates

Before You Read

Ask the children to think about the kinds of things they like to do on a snowy day. Tell them that you will read a story about what other people do when it snows. Have the children look to see if some of the things people in the story do are things they like to do.

After You Read

Briefly review the story by asking the children what things they do that were mentioned in the story. If you live in an area where there is little or no snow, ask the children if they think they would enjoy doing the things mentioned in the story. Then tell the children that there is a special kind of snowman they can make right in the classroom. Select a group of three or four children to make the snowmen.

You may want to prepare a recipe chart based on the cake mix you have. (For very young children, you may wish to use a mix for the frosting as well.) Follow the mix directions to make the cupcake batter. Coat the cups in the muffin tins with margarine and dust with flour. Spoon in the batter, filling each cup about halfway.

When the cupcakes are in the oven, assemble a second group of children to make the frosting. Help the children read and follow the recipe chart (see the suggestions at the beginning of this chapter).

After baking and cooling the cupcakes, give each child a cupcake cut into a top and bottom half. Place the two halves side by side on a plate with the cut sides down. Frost the cupcake halves. Have the children use the candies to decorate their snowmen.

Followup

Help the children prepare a recipe booklet to take home. Use a folded sheet of blue construction paper for the cover. Paste white circles on it to make a snowman design. Use crayons to design a face and hat. Mimeograph the recipe for the frosting and paste it inside the booklet.

You may also wish to read the following book to the children.

Briggs, Raymond
The Snowman
New York: Random House, 1978
A little boy makes a snowman who takes him on an adventure. Textless.

Misti

Teacher Resources

Aeschliman, Bonnie. *STEP BY STEP MICRO-WAVE COOKING FOR BOYS & GIRLS*
Nashville, Tenn: Ideals, 1985
A cookbook designed for use with kindergarten through seventh grade.

Crocker, Betty. *BETTY CROCKER'S COOK-BOOK FOR BOYS AND GIRLS*
Racine, Wis.: Western, 1984
Introduces basic cooking techniques and utensils. Includes simple, illustrated recipes for salads, breads, main dishes, desserts, and snacks.

Croft, Karen B. *THE GOOD FOR ME COOK-BOOK*
Palo Alto, Calif.: R & E Research, 1971
Recipes for nutritious foods for use with children ages three through twelve.

Edge, Nellie. *KINDERGARTEN COOKS*
Port Angeles, Wash.: Pen-Print, 1976
Recipes with illustrations.

Emerson, Anne. *PETER RABBIT'S COOKERY BOOK*
New York: Warne, 1986
Illustrated by Beatrix Potter.

Flemming, Bonnie Mack; Hamilton, Darlene Softley; and JoAnne Deal Hicks. *RESOURCES FOR CREATIVE TEACHING IN EARLY CHILDHOOD EDUCATION*
New York: Harcourt Brace Jovanovich, 1977
Includes a section on food preparation.

Glovach, Linda. *THE LITTLE WITCH'S BLACK MAGIC COOKBOOK*
Englewood Cliffs, N.J.: Prentice-Hall, 1972
Halloween party recipe ideas for cookies and punch.

Haas, Carolyn B., et al. *RECIPES FOR FUN & LEARNING: CREATIVE LEARNING ACTIVITIES FOR YOUNG CHILDREN*
Chicago: CBH Publishing, 1982
Designed for use with preschool through primary grades.

Loller, Sherry Garrison. *THE SUPER FOOD COOKBOOK FOR KIDS*
Takoma Park, Md., Washington, D.C.: Review & Herald, 1976
Recipes with humorous illustrations.

Paul, Aileen. *KIDS COOKING WITHOUT A STOVE: A COOKBOOK FOR YOUNG CHILDREN*
Santa Fe, N.M.: Sunstone Press, 1985
Easy-to-follow recipes for desserts, drinks, salads, sandwiches, snacks, and candies that require no cooking.

Wilms, Barbara. *CRUNCHY BANANAS AND OTHER GREAT RECIPES KIDS CAN COOK*
Layton, Utah: Gibbs M. Smith, 1984
Recipes with related learning experiences for children ages two through eight.

Children's Books

Adams, Adrienne. *A WOGGLE OF WITCHES*
New York: Charles Scribner's Sons, 1971; paperback, 1985
Witches gather on Halloween night to have a party. "Witches' brew" punch with fruit floating in it.

Barrett, Judith. *CLOUDY WITH A CHANCE OF MEATBALLS*
New York: Atheneum, 1978
A fantasy tale of a land where food falls from the sky. Meatballs or pea soup.

Calhoun, Mary. *THE HUNGRY LEPRECHAUN*
New York: William Morrow, 1962
A leprechaun helps Patrick O'Michael find potatoes when the people in Ireland are starving. Baked potatoes or potato soup.

DePaola, Tomie. *PANCAKES FOR BREAKFAST*
New York: Harcourt Brace Jovanovich, 1978
Picture book about a woman who wakes up wanting pancakes for breakfast. She has to go many places to gather the ingredients, only to have her pets eat the pancakes. Pancakes.

Devlin, Harry, and Wende Devlin. *CRANBERRY CHRISTMAS*
New York: Parents' Magazine Press, 1976; Macmillan reprint, 1980
Mr. Grape chases the town children from the skating pond, claiming that it is his property. Mr. Whiskers knows that he owns it, but cannot find the title until he is forced to clean his house for his sister's Christmas visit. The recipe for cranberry sauce is on the back cover of the book. Cranberry sauce.

Dr. Seuss. *GREEN EGGS AND HAM*
New York: Random House, paper and cassette, 1987
A humorous Seuss story with the refrain "green eggs and ham." Green eggs scrambled

Greenaway, Kate. *A APPLE PIE*
New York: Warne, 1886; 1987
Each letter of the alphabet is illustrated with a saying about apple pie. Printed from the original woodblocks engraved in 1886. Apple pie

Gurney, Nancy, and Eric Gurney. *THE KING, THE MICE, AND THE CHEESE*
New York: Random House, 1965
The king loves cheese, but the mice keep eating it. After several attempts to solve his problem, the king strikes a bargain with the mice and they all have cheese. Cheese-making or tasting

Krauss, Ruth. *THE CARROT SEED*
New York: Harper & Row, 1945; Scholastic Book Services, 1971
Even though his family teases him, a little boy plants carrot seeds and cares for them, in the belief that they will grow. He is rewarded with a huge carrot. Carrot sticks or carrot salad

Lobel, Arnold. *OWL AT HOME*
New York: Harper & Row, 1975; paperback, 1982; cassette, 1987
Five short stories about Owl. The first deals with winter and eating pea soup; another is about salty tea. An I-Can-Read book for beginning readers. Pea soup

Minarik, Else Holmelund. *LITTLE BEAR*
New York: Harper & Row, 1957; paperback, 1978; cassette, 1984
Four stories about Little Bear and his mother; one is about birthday soup. An I-Can-Read book. Soup

Ross, Tony. *STONE SOUP*
New York: Dial Press, 1987
A version of the folktale about making stone soup. Vegetable soup

Sendak, Maurice. *IN THE NIGHT KITCHEN*
New York: Harper & Row, 1970; paperback, 1985
Mickey is suddenly awakened by a racket in the night. He falls through the dark and into the cake batter of the night kitchen. After pounding the dough into an airplane, he flies off to the Milky Way and gets all the milk the bakers need for the cake. Bread, biscuits, or cakes

DRAMA

Expression

Dramatization of stories and experiences is a natural part of early childhood education programs. Dramatic activities offer children opportunities to express themselves creatively and assume other roles in non-threatening situations. Such activities provide an outlet for emotions in a constructive manner and help children become aware of the feelings of others. Dramatic activities also develop language, memory, and sequencing skills and encourage children to develop their imaginations and thinking processes.

Dramatic play is encouraged through housekeeping and dress-up centers. The use of props by teachers can motivate children to express their feelings and interests through drama. Props for dramatization may include masks, clothing, handpuppets, finger puppets, stick puppets, and flannelboard characters.

Literary experiences often lead to creative expression through dramatization. The child learns through imitation and actively assuming the roles he or she has seen portrayed. Most dramatic experiences for young children are informal in nature and do not require the memorization of lines.

Even without prompting, children will dramatize incidents from stories they have heard. When children have seen a flannelboard story presented, they naturally wish to use the characters to tell the story themselves. They can remember the sequence of events and often model the language they have heard or expressions they have seen. Often, too, children want to perform their own versions of a story using the same characters.

The use of masks and costumes aids the shy or quiet child in assuming a different role. Behind a mask, the child may confidently undertake a role that he or she would not portray in reality. A child's hidden concerns and feelings may be expressed through extemporaneous dialogue and actions in dramatic experiences.

Using Flannelboard Characters

Many stories have dramatization potential. Stories with few characters lend themselves particularly well to flannelboard presentation. Many wordless texts also can be effectively told using flannelboard characters.

Outlines are provided in appendix C to help you make flannelboard figures for the activities in this chapter. Trace or draw the outline on felt, then cut out the figure.

Flannelboard figures may be decorated on both sides by gluing on smaller felt details or by drawing details with marking pens. Figures that are detailed on both sides allow greater flexibility for storytelling.

Flannelboard figures can also be made by cutting out pictures from an old or inexpensive book. Paste felt on the picture backs and cover the fronts with clear contact paper to protect them.

Pictures from coloring books may also be suitable for making flannelboard characters. Color them, cover with clear contact paper, cut them out, then glue felt or flocked paper on the backs.

Familiarize yourself with story sequences before using flannelboard figures to illustrate them. You may wish to practice placing the figures on the flannelboard before you tell the story to the children.

Activities

Barrett, John. *THE LITTLEST MULE*
Silver Dollar City, Mo.: Silver Dollar City, 1977
Homer, an inventor, and Rufus, a very small mule, are always being made fun
of, but together they invent a merry-go-round that brings happiness to others.

Materials

- six 12-inch sticks or rulers
- cutout figures of Homer, Rufus, the landlady, Mary Beth, Jimmy, and the town banker (see appendix C, pages 133-34)

Before You Read

Construct the six stick puppets of the characters in the story. You may wish to use the outlines in the appendix C, pages 133-34. Cut the figures out of cardboard and color in features. Attach the figures to sticks to be used as handles.

Arrange the children in a semicircle for the reading of the story. Choose six children to hold the stick puppets. Be sure to position the children so they can see each other and the book.

Tell the children with the puppets that they will have to listen very carefully. Explain that each time their character speaks in the story they should hold the puppet up for all to see. When the character is not speaking, they should keep the puppet lowered, face down, to the floor.

Read the story as the children use the puppets. If necessary, subtly prompt the children with nonverbal gestures to hold up their puppets at the correct times.

After You Read

Discuss with the children how Rufus and Homer showed their friendship for each other. Ask the children to tell you what *caring* means and to describe how they act when they care about someone. Ask them to describe how they treat their friends.

Followup

Cut out additional cardboard puppet figures and let the children color in their own features and clothing. Have the children act out plays using the figures.

Spread out a large piece of drawing paper on the floor. Have the children draw a mural of the events at the fair described in *The Littlest Mule*.

Berg, Jean (retold by). *THE LITTLE RED HEN*
Chicago: Follett, 1963
An old British folktale about a hen who tries to get the other animals in the
barnyard to help her plant wheat to make bread. They refuse to help, but she
has the last laugh when the bread is baked.

Materials

- paper sacks
- scraps of colored construction paper
- crayons
- scissors
- glue

Before You Read

Tell the children that the story you will read is an old folktale that their parents or grandparents may have enjoyed when they were children.

After You Read

Briefly discuss the animal characters in the story. Ask the children which characters they would like to be, in a play about the little red hen. Have each child choose a character to portray.

Show the children a sack mask you have made depicting one of the characters. Tell the children you will help them make masks like the characters they have chosen. Discuss the features that the children may want to put on the masks. Using paper sacks with precut eye holes, help the children design their masks by cutting out and pasting on ears, beaks, mouths, and other features, and coloring the sacks.

When the puppets are finished, have the children re-enact the story of the little red hen or a story of their own. You may want to reread the story and have the children act out the parts of the characters as you read.

Followup

Discuss how flour is made and what it is used for. Mix up dough and bake a loaf of bread. This may be done in an electric fry pan or portable roaster if no stove is available.

Visit a bakery and watch bread being made.

Dramatize other adventures of the little red hen that the children or you think of.

Spier, Peter. *FOOD MARKET*
Peter Spier's Village Board Book, 1981
This is a board shape book showing the things in a food market.

Materials

- play money
- toy cash register or paper cups or muffin tin
- small sale items (packaged) or empty food containers
- price signs
- a table of boxes for a checkout stand

Before You Read

Ask the children if they have ever helped shop for groceries in a food store. Discuss the variety of food stores and the shopping procedures in a large market. Show the children the cover of the book first, and discuss what is different about it (the shape). Next, read through and look at the book together.

After You Read

Ask the children what things are needed to have a store. Plan a make-believe market. Set up an area to display items for sale such as small packages of crackers or raisins or even empty food boxes. Help the children make price signs. Use a table or boxes to set up a checkout stand. Talk about where the money is kept in a grocery. If you have a toy cash register, you may wish to use it. If not, make a cash register using paper cups or a muffin tin for sorting.

Choose children to be checkers and sackers. Distribute play money to other children who will be the shoppers. Have the children select their goods and pay for them at the checkout stand. Use the checkout stand process to explain the need for money and how to make change.

Let the children continue to operate the market daily for a week. Change roles of customers and market workers. Discuss good manners at the store.

Followup

Visit a nearby food market with a list of items to buy. Select the items and pay for them at the checkout stand. Write a language experience story about your classroom supermarket or a trip to a real market.

You might also wish to discuss how the food gets to the market and where the food comes from.

Galdone, Paul (illustr.). *THE THREE LITTLE PIGS*
New York: Houghton Mifflin; paperback, 1984
Each of the three pigs builds a house, but when the wolf comes to call, only
the house made of brick offers protection.

Materials

- flannelboard
- flannelboard figures (see appendix C, pages 135-36)

Before You Read

Construct the flannelboard figures needed for telling the story. If you wish, refer to the beginning of
this chapter and the outlines on pages 135 and 136 for help in constructing the flannelboard figures. Introduce the story by telling the children that you will tell them an old folktale, one they may have heard before.
Use the flannelboard figures to illustrate the story of the three pigs as you tell it to the children. Encourage
the children to join you in saying the refrains: "Not by the hair of my chinny, chin, chin" and "Then I'll
huff, and I'll puff, and I'll blow your house in."

After You Read

Ask the children for volunteers to help retell the story. Choose children to play the three pigs and the
wolf. Let them practice retelling the story before presenting it to the other children.

Let the children retell the story using the flannelboard figures. Encourage the children to think of new
endings for the story of the three pigs or make up new stories using the same figures.

Ginsburg, Mirra. *THE CHICK AND THE DUCKLING*
New York: Macmillan, 1972
A chick tries to do everything that a duckling does. The difference in their
abilities is clear when the duckling has to pull the chick out of the water. (Trans-
lated from Russian.)

Materials

- flannelboard
- flannelboard figures (see appendix C, page 137)

Before You Read

Construct the flannelboard figures needed for telling the story. If you wish, refer to the beginning of
this chapter and the outlines on page 137 for help in constructing flannelboard figures. Use the flannelboard
figures to illustrate the story of the chick and the duckling as you read it to the children.

After You Read

Ask for volunteers to retell the story using the flannelboard figures. The other children may participate
by telling what event will occur next.

Discuss with the children what might have happened if the duckling had tried to do everything that the
chick did. Encourage the children to think of a new story based on this idea and use the flannelboard figures
to illustrate it.

Keep the flannelboard and figures available for future use and retelling of the story. Encourage the
children to create their own stories using the figures.

Followup

Teach the children the song "Old MacDonald Had a Farm" and have them imitate chick and duckling sounds.

Discuss the differences among animals and their different abiliies. Ask the children if they think humans have different abilities too. If so, what kinds?

Crews, Donald. *FREIGHT TRAIN*
New York: Greenwillow Books, 1978
A simply drawn picture book which illustrates the travels of a freight train while identifying types of cars and colors. The limited text is in large print for ease of reading.

Materials

- flannelboard
- flannelboard figures (see appendix C, pages 138-40)

Before You Read

Construct the flannelboard figures needed for telling the story. If you wish, refer to the beginning of this chapter and the outlines on pages 138-40 for help in constructing flannelboard figures. Use the flannelboard and figures to tell the story.

After You Read

Ask for volunteers to retell the story of the train's journey using the flannelboard figures and making sound effects. Encourage children to introduce the characters by identifying the color and name of the type of car. Allow them to refer to the storybook if necessary.

Keep the flannelboard and figures available for future use. Encourage children to create their own stories using the figures or by combining them with characters from other stories.

Followup

Collect pictures of trains and make a bulletin-board display. Set up a model train.

Other concept books by Crews that may be of interest follow.

Carousel
New York: Greenwillow Books, 1982

Parade
New York: Greenwillow Books, 1983

Truck
New York: Greenwillow Books, 1980

Keats, Ezra Jack. *PET SHOW!*
New York: Macmillan, 1972; paperback, 1974
A boy wants to enter a cat in a pet show, but the cat runs away. Then the boy discovers a very unusual pet to enter — a germ in a jar.

Materials

- stuffed animal toys
- cardboard or heavy paper
- colored ribbon or paper strips
- tape, safety pins, or string

Before You Read

Allow at least two days for this activity. The first day, read the story and plan and practice for the pet show. Begin by asking the children if any of them has ever attended a pet show. If so, ask him or her to tell about it. If not, ask the children what they think might happen at a pet show. Then tell the children that you will read a story about a pet show.

After You Read

Discuss with the children what happened at the pet show. Tell the children that they can have a pet show, too. However, the pets they will show will be stuffed animal toys, not live animals. Briefly discuss why you cannot use real pets in this show. (If a child indicates that he or she does not have a toy pet, that child may want to assist the judges or draw a make-believe pet.)

Explain to the children that the judges of the pet show will want to know the pet's name and something about it, such as where the child got it, or how old it is. Then tell the children that they will practice for the show. Form the class into a circle. One at a time, have each child step to the center of the circle. The child should say the pet's name and something about it. If necessary, ask the child questions to learn something about the pet. After the child has told about his or her pet, he or she should walk around the circle pretending to show the pet to the judges and other show participants. You may want to play march music as the child shows the pet.

Ask the children to tell you what items they think they will need for the pet show. Guide the children to suggest judges, pets, and awards. Tell them that name badges may also be used.

Use the cardboard or heavy paper to make name badges. Help the children print their names and those of their pets on the badges. The children may decorate their badges and put them away for the show.

Have a small group of children make the awards. Make circles about 2 inches in diameter from the cardboard or heavy paper. Glue on paper strips or ribbons about 6 inches long. Have the children decorate the awards. Secure the badges or awards to clothing with loops of tape, safety pins, or string run through a hole in the badge or award. Make up enough award ribbons for each child to receive one. Wait to make up the winning categories until the show.

Send a note home to parents asking them to let the children bring a stuffed animal toy to school. Be sure to specify *toy* rather than live animals.

On the day of the pet show, review how the show is to be held. After the children have shown their pets, the judges should award ribbons for such categories as "longest legs," "biggest eyes," "softest fur," and so forth. Judges may include other teachers and adults, as well as the children. Children who help judge should also get ribbons for their assistance.

Followup

Have the children dictate a story about the pet show. Write the text on chart paper and illustrate it.

Milne, A. A. *WINNIE THE POOH*
New York: E. P. Dutton, 1926, 1971, 1974; Dell, paperback, 1970, 1984
The adventures of Winnie the Pooh, a stuffed bear, and other toy animals belonging to Christopher Robin.

Materials

- old, white bedsheet, white cloth, or white socks
- stapler, or needles and thread
- scissors
- crayons or marking pens

Before You Read

Briefly explain the main characters in the story to the children. Choose one episode to read.

After You Read

Tell the children that they can make hand puppets to represent the characters in the story, and that they can use the puppets to retell the episode they just heard about.

For very young children, you may wish to make puppets from old socks instead of cloth. Explain to the children that they should draw the face on the toe of the sock. Demonstrate how to place the sock flat on the table with the toe at the top.

Older children may make puppets from white or lightly colored cloth or bedsheets. Have the children fold the cloth so that it is doubled. Next, the children should place their hands on the cloth and loosely trace around their thumbs, three middle fingers together, and little finger. Explain that the outline must be larger than their hands so that seams can be sewn or stapled.

The doubled cloth is then cut along the traced line. You may need to help the children cut the cloth. When the cloth has been cut, the children may decorate their hand puppets using crayons or marking pens to draw the features of the character of their choosing from the story. The sides of the puppets may then be fastened together by sewing or stapling the edges.

Discuss with the children why they chose the character they did. Then have them act out part of the story using their puppets.

Followup

Have the children use their puppets to perform a class play. A puppet stage may be constructed from a shipping crate or cardboard box. Children may want to create their own stories and additional characters. You may suggest other animal stories for them to portray.

Dr. Seuss. *HORTON HATCHES THE EGG*
New York: Random House, 1940
Horton, an elephant, agrees to sit on lazy Mayzie's egg while she takes a rest.
Horton sits through hot and cold, rain and snow, and other trials while Mayzie
enjoys herself.

Before You Read

Ask the children if they know what it means to be faithful. Discuss their ideas. Then tell them that you are going to read a story about an elephant named Horton who means what he says.

After You Read

Ask the children how it must have felt for Horton to wait all of that time up in a tree on a limb through all kinds of weather. Discuss what it means to be faithful and how Horton demonstrated it. Talk about why the story is funny and if it could really happen.

Tell the children that you want them to pretend to be Horton and act out the things that Horton does. Tell them that you will go first. Pantomime an event such as climbing the tree and settling on the nest. As the children pretend, give verbal hints such as "A terrible storm has come up and rain is falling in your eyes."

Encourage children to use facial expressions to show whether the event is pleasant or unpleasant. Ask for other volunteers to act out the parts of the taunting animals, Mayzie, the hunters, and so on. You might read the text as children pantomime their parts.

Silverstein, Shel. *THE GIVING TREE*
New York: Harper & Row, 1964
From childhood through manhood, a boy returns to an old apple tree to ask it
for gifts. Each time, the tree responds, until it is only a stump.

Materials

- flannelboard
- flannelboard figures (see appendix C, pages 141-42)

Before You Read

Construct your flannelboard tree figure in sections so that you have a stump, a piece of trunk, branches, leaves, and apples. If you wish, refer to the beginning of this chapter and the outlines on pages 141 and 142 for help in constructing flannelboard figures. Use the flannelboard figures to illustrate the story of the tree as you tell it to the children.

After You Read

Briefly review the events of the story. Then select two children to retell the story using the flannelboard figures while you read from the book. Next, have the children tell the story as other children use the flannelboard figures.

Discuss with the children the meaning of the word *generous*.

Followup

Re-enact the story as a play. Use props of a hat, coat, and cane to demonstrate the boy growing older.

Make a chart of the many products we receive from trees. Create a language experience story chart about apple trees. See the beginning of chapter 6, "Language Development," for hints on creating a language experience chart.

Marshall, James. *GEORGE AND MARTHA ENCORE*
Boston: Houghton Mifflin, 1973
George and Martha are good friends. In this book there are five short stories.
In the fourth story, "At the Beach," Martha does not listen to George's advice
about the sun.

Materials

- flannelboard
- flannelboard figures (see appendix C, pages 143-44)

Before You Read

Construct the flannelboard figures needed for telling the story. If you wish, refer to the beginning of
this chapter and the outlines on pages 143-44 for help in constructing flannelboard figures. Show the children
the figures of George and Martha and tell their names. Explain that they are good friends. Tell them you
will read a story about the friends. Use the flannelboard figures to illustrate the story as you read it to the
children.

After You Read

Tell the children that they can make their own flannelboard figures. For older children, have cardboard
patterns of the animals available for them to trace. Have the children trace the patterns onto construction
paper. After tracing, have them cut out the figures and draw in their features. Then have them glue flocked
paper or pieces of felt to the backs of the figures. (Flocked paper may be obtained from wallpaper sample
books.)

For younger children, have the two main characters precut from construction paper. Let the children
draw and cut out the tree, water, and beach from construction paper. Have the children draw features on
their characters. Next, have them glue pieces of flocked paper or felt on the backs.

As each child completes his or her set of figures, he or she can retell the story using the flannelboard.

Followup

Encourage the children to create a new story using their characters.
Have the children take their figures home and re-enact the story for their families.

Other books about George and Martha which are written by James Marshall and which might be of interest are listed below.

George and Martha
Boston: Houghton Mifflin, 1972

George and Martha Back in Town
Boston: Houghton Mifflin, 1984

George and Martha One Fine Day
Boston: Houghton Mifflin, 1978

Sendak, Maurice. ***WHERE THE WILD THINGS ARE***
New York: Harper & Row, 1963; paperback, 1984; Scholastic Book Services, 1988
When Max is sent to his room without his supper, he begins to imagine wild things. He journeys off and away to the land of the wild things where he romps and plays with them before deciding to return home.

Before You Read

Ask the children if someone has ever called them a *wild thing*, perhaps when they were playing loudly or racing about. Tell the children that the story you will read is about a boy who has been sent to his room without his supper for acting like a wild thing.

After You Read

Ask the children to tell you what *pretending* or *imagining* means. Ask them if they think Max really sailed away to a place where wild things are. Talk about the things children enjoy pretending or imagining. Then tell the children that they are going to play a pretending game.

Start the pretending game with a make-believe lump of clay. Explain to the children that they can make anything they want out of the clay. Demonstrate by working the make-believe clay into a shape. You might shape the clay into a square of bubble gum, place it in your mouth, and pretend to blow a bubble. Then ask the children to tell you what you made.

When the children have guessed what you made, pass the make-believe clay to a child and have him or her shape something. Have the other children guess what it is. Continue until all the children who wish to try have had turns.

Followup

Use a costume ring to play a game of make-believe. Tell the children that when you place the "magic ring" on your finger and wish, you become whomever or whatever you wish to be.

Demonstrate for the children. Place the ring on your finger, look thoughtful for a moment, then act out the part of the person, animal, or thing you wish to be. For example, you may pretend to be a cat and wash your face with your "paws." Have the children guess who or what you are. Then pass the ring to a child in the circle. Let each child have a chance to pretend. If necessary, ask the children questions to help establish their make-believe identities.

Zolotow, Charlotte. *WILLIAM'S DOLL*
New York: Harper & Row, 1972
William wanted a doll, but his father and others did not want him to have it.
He was called a sissy. His grandmother solves the problem by getting him a
doll and explaining that William is practicing to be a father.

Before You Read

Tell the children that you will read them a story about a boy who wanted a doll for a toy though some people did not think it was right. As you read the story, use motions suggested by the text such as shooting a basketball, cuddling a doll, and making a figure eight for the train track.

After You Read

Briefly discuss with the children the idea of William wanting a doll for a toy. Ask the children to tell you about the toys they enjoy playing with.

Ask the children to think of their favorite toy, but not to say what it is. Tell them that you will give them the chance to tell what it is without using words.

Explain the meaning of *pantomime* and pantomime the use of a toy for the children. Then let each child have the chance to pantomime the use of his or her favorite toy. Have the other children guess what they think the toy is. You may need to ask questions to help the children guess. You may wish to have the child who guesses correctly do the next pantomime, or allow the turns to proceed around the circle.

Teacher Resources

Bauer, Caroline Feller. *HANDBOOK FOR STORYTELLERS*
Chicago: American Library Association, 1977
Includes a section on creative dramatics.

Day, Barbara. *EARLY CHILDHOOD EDUCATION: CREATIVE LEARNING ACTIVITIES*, 3d ed.
New York: Macmillan, 1988
A textbook that deals with aspects of creative activities for early childhood.

Day, Barbara. *OPEN LEARNING IN EARLY CHILDHOOD*
New York: Macmillan, 1975
Includes a chapter on creative dramatics, with a description of objectives and suggested materials.

Kay, Drina. *ALL THE DESK'S A STAGE*
Nashville, Tenn.: Incentive Publications, 1982
Information on use of drama.

Luckin, Joyce. *EASY-TO-MAKE PUPPETS*
Boston: Plays, 1975
Instructions and patterns for making twenty-four different puppets.

Miller, Helen L. *EVERYDAY PLAYS FOR BOYS & GIRLS*
Dunmore, Pa.: Plays, 1986
Plays for use in drama.

Stewig, John W. *SPONTANEOUS DRAMA: A LANGUAGE ART*
Columbus, Ohio: Charles E. Merrill, 1973
A description of what *spontaneous drama* is, how to produce it, and the need for it in the elementary classroom.

Williams, DeAtna M. *PAPER-BAG PUPPETS*
Belmont, Calif.: D. S. Lake, 1968
Additional puppet projects.

Children's Books

Briggs, Raymond. *THE SNOWMAN*
New York: Random House, 1978
This is a textless book about a boy who builds a snowman. The snowman later flies off on an adventure with the boy and returns. The next day when the boy goes outside, the snowman has melted away.

Carrier, Lark. *A CHRISTMAS PROMISE*
Natick, Maine: Picture Book Studio, 1986
Christmas is coming and Amy makes the animals leave her tree. When all of the animals are gone and the tree is bare, she realizes how much she misses them and asks them to come back. They do and they decorate the tree.

Charlip, Remy. *FORTUNATELY*
New York: Macmillan, 1964; reprint, 1985
A boy is invited to a party. Unfortunately, he is in one city and the party in another. Fortunately, he borrows a plane, but unfortunately, he has engine trouble. This story continues in this alternating pattern of fortunate and unfortunate events.

DeRegniers, Beatrice. *MAY I BRING A FRIEND?*
New York: Atheneum, 1964; paperback, 1974
A king and queen invite a boy to tea, and he asks if he can bring a friend. Each time he comes to tea, he brings a different animal friend.

Galdone, Paul. *THE THREE BILLY GOATS GRUFF*
New York: Houghton Mifflin, 1981
Galdone's version of this traditional tale.

Grimm, Jacob, and Wilhelm Grimm.
SNOW WHITE AND THE SEVEN DWARFS: A TALE FROM THE BROTHERS GRIMM
New York: Farrar, Straus & Giroux, 1972
A wicked witch casts a spell on Snow White, who is later awakened by the kiss of a handsome prince.

Newton, Laura P. *WILLIAM THE VEHICLE KING*
New York: Macmillan-Bradbury, 1987
William begins playing imaginatively in his room with all sorts of vehicles. Gradually other toys and blocks become a part of the landscape.

Spier, Peter. *PETER SPIER'S RAIN.*
New York: Doubleday, 1982; paperback, 1987
In this wordless picture book, all of the scenes and aspects of a rainstorm are seen from the start to the clearing with sun returning.

Williams, Barbara. *ALBERT'S TOOTHACHE*
New York: E. P. Dutton, 1974
No one believes that Albert, a turtle, has a toothache. His grandmother discovers that his "toothache" is really in his toe.

LANGUAGE DEVELOPMENT

Literature

Acquisition of language and the improvement of language skills are major concerns of early childhood education programs. Literary experiences can be catalysts for language development. Research has shown a positive relationship between children's levels of verbal ability and their early experiences with literature, that is, in having been read to.

Reading to young children or telling them stories provides children with speech models. It enables children to improve their vocabularies. It helps children become familiar with sentence patterns and word arrangements. It provides examples of pronunciation and language rhythm. Reading to children also broadens their awareness and knowledge of concepts.

Stories also stimulate children to verbally express their feelings and beliefs. Children who are given opportunities to speak and are encouraged to do so can improve their language skills through practice.

Picture stories are particularly effective in motivating children to speak. As the meaning of the picture story develops, children are motivated to share their insights. If a child fails to comprehend an aspect of a story, it is easy to review the pictures or draw attention to details.

Some wordless stories may be used to create language experience charts. The children see the story, talk about it, and then dictate a story about it. The language experience charts may then be used for "reading" together. In this manner, children are experiencing the association between print and speaking. The idea that printed words are "talk" written down is being conveyed.

Language Experience Stories

Language experience stories are stories that children create using their own language. Such stories are dictated by the children to the teacher, who writes them down. This activity is usually most successful with a small group of children, perhaps eight or fewer, so that all of the children have an opportunity to take part. Whenever possible, it is advisable to create language experience stories or sentences with just one child. As the child dictates, write down the words on the chalkboard, chart paper, or child's drawing paper. (Stories originally written on the chalkboard can be copied on chart paper for later use.) Often language experience activities may be motivated by a drawing that the child wishes to talk about. Or, the class or a group may want to dictate a story about a field trip.

After you have recorded the story, and the children have created a title for it, reread the story to the group or child involved. As you say the words, point to the written words on the chart. After the first complete reading of the chart, return to the title and ask the children to read it with you. First point to and say the words. Then ask the children to read with you as you again point to the words and say them aloud.

After the chart has been read by you and by the children, ask for volunteers to come to the chart and find words that begin with the same letters as their names. You may frame a word using your hands and ask for a volunteer to try to find another word just like it. Have the child frame that word with his or her own hands. You may also review punctuation marks with the children by pointing to a period or comma and asking what it is called or what it means.

Further activities with language experience charts may include making copies of the sentences on sentence strip paper and having the children find the sentence on the chart that matches the sentence strip. Another activity is to have the children arrange the sentence strips in the order of their appearance in the story to develop concepts of sequencing. Sentence strips may also be cut up into individual words. Ask the children to match the word strip with the same word on the chart.

For very young children, who have not yet demonstrated an interest in reading, not all of the afore-mentioned activities are appropriate. For some preschool children, the teacher may wish only to develop the concept of the relationship between print and speech. For more advanced children, language experience can be used to teach such skills as left-to-right progression, sequencing, sight word vocabulary, configuration clues in word recognition, word boundaries, and punctuation.

Many prereading and reading skills can be taught through the use of language experience charts. It is an effective means for teaching beginning reading and remedial reading because the personal nature of the material is self-motivating. It should be cautioned, however, that language experience charts should not be forced on a child who has not yet demonstrated readiness. For the child who is motivated to begin working with printed words, the language experience approach provides an informal, subtle, and interesting start in reading.

Activities

Baylor, Byrd. *EVERYBODY NEEDS A ROCK*
New York: Charles Scribner's Sons, 1974
How to find a rock that is "not just any rock ... a special rock that you find yourself and keep as long as you can—maybe forever."

Materials

- a rock
- chart paper
- crayon or marker pen

Before You Read

If possible, obtain a rock with attractive features or markings to show the children. Point out that some people collect rocks that are attractive or unusual. Ask the children if any of them has ever collected rocks or kept one that was special in some way. Tell them that you will read a book about how to find special rocks.

After You Read

Tell the children that you will take them outside to look for special rocks. Tell them that each of them should try to find a special rock.

Take the children to a place on the school grounds where rocks may be found. After each child has a rock, take the rocks back to the classroom. Have the children wash them off and dry them.

Tell the children that they will write a story about their rock hunt. Ask the children for suggestions about how to start. You may need to prompt them by asking what they did first, what they did next, and so forth. After the children have dictated the beginning of the story, you might suggest that each child show his or her rock to the group and describe it in a complete sentence. Write the sentences down on the experience chart.

When the chart is complete, read it back to the children, pointing to the words as you do so. After reading each sentence or phrase, encourage the children to repeat the statement with you as you say it a second time.

You may wish to refer to the beginning of this chapter for additional suggestions on using language experience stories.

Followup

Have the children set up a rock display for the classroom.
Let the children draw pictures to illustrate their language experience story.

Carle, Eric. *THE VERY BUSY SPIDER*
New York: Putnam, 1985
A simple story which uses raised lines to show a spider spinning her web.

Materials

- chart paper
- crayon or marker pen

Before You Read

Ask the children if they have ever watched a spider making a web. Briefly discuss the variety of spiderwebs and the concept that each spider makes its own distinctive kind of web. Tell the children that you are going to share a book with them which is about a spider spinning her web. Point out that they will want to look carefully at the pictures and may wish to feel the lines later.

After You Read

Return to the beginning of the book and ask volunteers to help you retell the story. Write down the children's story as they dictate it. You may want to write it first on the chalkboard and later copy it onto the chart paper. You may wish to refer to the beginning of this chapter for additional suggestions on using language experience stories.

Followup

Use string and glue to create a spiderweb on paper. Draw a friendly spider on the web.
Form plasticene (clay) balls to make the body of a spider. Attach 8 pipe cleaners for legs. Use different colored clay or two beads to form eyes.

Hutchins, Pat. *TITCH*
New York: Macmillan, 1971
Titch, the little brother of Mary and Pete, always gets a smaller toy than his brother and sister. However, Titch plants a seed that grows very large.

Materials

- paper cups (one per child)
- pebbles
- potting soil
- seeds
- crayons or marking pens

Before You Read

Tell the children that you will read them a story about a boy who was upset because he always got smaller toys than his bigger brother and sister. Ask the children to look for how he solved his problem.

After You Read

Briefly review the story with the children. Ask them to tell you what was so surprising about Titch's seed. Tell the children that they will have a chance to try what Titch did.

Discuss with the children the things a plant needs to grow. Then give each child a paper cup. If the cups do not have a waxy surface, the children may want to decorate them with crayons or marking pens. Write each child's name on the bottom of his or her cup with permanent marking pen.

Explain to the children step by step how to plant the seeds.

Steps

1. Place a layer of pebbles in the bottom of the cup.

2. Put soil in the cup to within 1 inch (demonstrate this measurement) of the top.

3. Poke a hole in the soil using your finger.

4. Drop a seed in the hole and push soil over it.

5. Give the seed a small drink of water using a spoon.

Place the cups on a sunny windowsill. Have the children keep a chart of how many days it takes for the seeds to sprout. They may also want to keep a watering chart to be sure each plant is cared for.

Followup

Have the children dictate a chart describing the steps in planting the seeds. Make a copy of the chart for each child and have the children illustrate each step.

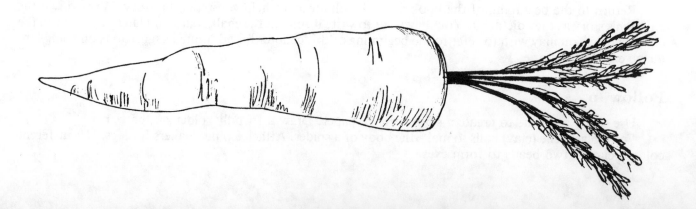

Spier, Peter. *NOAH'S ARK*
New York: Doubleday, 1977; paperback, 1981
This is the biblical story of Noah's ark told with detailed, sometimes slightly
humorous, pictures. There is no text except for the opening poem.

Before You Read

Tell the children that you will share a picture book together about the story of Noah's ark.

After You Read

Ask the children to retrace the development of the story: What happened first in the story (the building of the ark)? What were some of the animals that got into the ark? How did Noah know that the flood was receding?

Tell the children that they are to think of an animal that got into the ark and pretend to be that animal. Have the children volunteer to pretend to be their choice of animal while the others try to name it. Let the children take turns pretending and guessing. If the children cannot guess an animal by the pretender's actions, the child should give verbal hints or respond to the other children's yes-or-no questions. You may wish to demonstrate the game or begin it by pretending to be a rabbit. If children do not guess the animal by your hopping actions, then give hints such as "I have long ears."

Lauren

Followup

Let each child draw or paint a picture of an animal that got on the ark and dictate a few sentences about it. Use modeling clay to make animals, the ark, and Noah's family. Set up a display around the book. Make a display of other books by Peter Spier such as *Peter Spier's Rain* or *Peter Spier's Christmas!* Talk about the kinds of illustrations that Peter Spier draws. How are they alike?

Spier, Peter. *PETER SPIER'S CHRISTMAS!*
New York: Doubleday, 1983
This is a wordless detailed picture book about the events preceding, during, and after Christmas. The pictures express the anticipation and customs involved in the Christmas celebration.

Before You Read

Ask the children what holiday is going to happen soon. Then ask them to tell you some of the things they do in their homes to get ready for Christmas. Tell the children that you are going to look at a book together. Announce the title and explain that Peter Spier is the person who drew the pictures or illustrations and thought of this picture story. Carefully display the pages so that all can see them.

After You Read

Ask the children to tell what things people do before Christmas that were shown in the story. Then discuss what events happen at Christmas, and finally, what happens after Christmas is over. After general discussion about the book and pictures, ask the children to dictate a story to go with the book. Write this story on the chalkboard and later transfer to chart paper. (*Note*: There are suggestions for techniques to use in writing language experience stories at the beginning of this chapter.) Have a few children draw small pictures on the chart to illustrate various words.

Followup

Draw scenes of the events that happen before, during, and after Christmas. Display these with the book done with subtitles by the children.

Kellogg, Steven. *MUCH BIGGER THAN MARTIN*
New York: Dial Press, 1976; paperback, 1978
Martin's younger brother dreams and imagines what it would be like to be bigger than Martin. He tries to find ways to be bigger than Martin. This is a humorous story about the feelings of a little brother in his relationship with his older, bigger brother.

Before You Read

Ask how many of the children have brothers or sisters. Find out in which cases the child in your class is the older sibling and in which he or she is the youngest. Then tell the children that you are going to read a story about a boy who has an older brother.

After You Read

Ask the children how Martin's brother felt about being the youngest. What could Martin do that his younger brother could not? Ask the children about situations in their lives. If they are younger, do they sometimes wish they could do things that an older sibling does? If there is a baby in the family, ask the children to describe how they can help with the baby because of the things a baby cannot do. Ask the children to remember some of the things they could not do when they were younger. Discuss their "growing up" and the things that make people change. What are some of the signs the children may have noticed that indicate their growth? (needing larger clothes, being able to write their names, walking home alone, riding a bicycle, etc.)

Followup

Have the children dictate a list of things they can do and draw pictures or find them in magazines to illustrate these skills.

Kellogg, Steven. *THE MYSTERIOUS TADPOLE*
New York: Dial Press, 1977; paperback, 1979
Every year for his birthday Louis receives a gift for his nature collection from his uncle in Scotland. This year the gift is what appears to be a small tadpole in a jar. However, the tadpole grows and grows and becomes very large. It is only with the help of a librarian that a solution to the problem of where to "house" the gift is found.

Before You Read

Ask the children if they have ever received any unusual gifts for birthday presents. Discuss their responses briefly. Then tell them that you are going to read a story about a boy named Louis who got a mysterious gift for his birthday. Talk about the word *mysterious* and what it means.

After You Read

Ask the children if they would like to receive a gift like the tadpole that Louis got from his uncle. Ask what they might do with it or what they think their parents might say about it. Discuss whether this story could really happen. Tell the children about the tales of the Loch Ness monster and where it is supposed to live. You might use a globe or map to explain how far away the place is. Finally, ask about the ending of the story. What do the children think might come from Louis's uncle's latest gift?

Followup

Draw a picture or describe verbally what might develop from the latest gift.

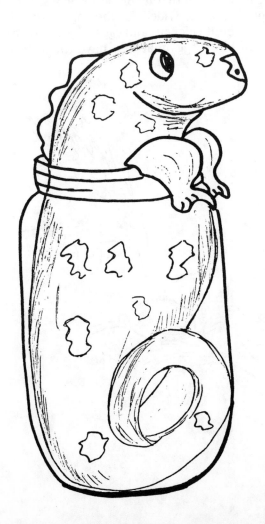

Kent, Jack. *THE EGG BOOK*
New York: Macmillan, 1975

A hen watches as another hen hatches an egg. The first hen goes out looking for an egg of her own to hatch. However, each time the hen finds an egg, an animal other than a chick emerges. Finally, the hen finds the right egg.

Before You Read

Ask the children what are some of the animals that live on the farm. Guide the discussion toward chickens, and where they come from. Tell the children that you are going to share a book with them that is about a chicken. Display the book and read the title to them.

After You Read

Return to the beginning of the book and discuss the kinds of eggs the chicken found. Talk about the animals that are hatched from eggs. Ask how the eggs are different and if only birds lay eggs. Ask the children if any of them has ever watched eggs being hatched. If so, discuss experiences. Make a chart of the different animals that hatch from eggs.

Followup

Take a field trip to a hatchery and have the children dictate a language experience story about it.

Hatch chicken eggs in your classroom. Small inexpensive two-egg hatchers may be purchased from teachers' supply catalogues or may be made using a styrofoam box, electric light, and thermometer. Hatcheries can often supply eggs at various stages of development so that you need not wait the full period for incubation of the eggs. Time the hatching so that it will occur on a school day, if possible. You will need to keep in mind that a home will need to be provided for the chicks after hatching.

A display of informational books about chickens and eggs might also be set up in the classroom interest center. Children might bring pieces of birds' eggs that they have found to include in a science display.

Marshall, James. *GEORGE AND MARTHA*
Boston: Houghton Mifflin, 1972; paperback, 1974

Marshall, James. *GEORGE AND MARTHA ENCORE*
Boston: Houghton Mifflin, 1973; paperback, 1977
Four short stories about the friendship between George and Martha, two hippopotamuses.

Before You Read

Show the children a picture of George and Martha from the book. Ask the children to tell you what kind of animal they are. Then tell the children that you will read them a story about the two hippopotamuses George and Martha, who are very good friends.

After You Read

Ask the children how they think George and Martha felt about each other. How can the children tell that George and Martha are friends?
Discuss the meaning of *friendship*. Ask the children to talk about how they act with their friends. Ask the children if they have ever been angry with a friend. If so, why? Ask the children to tell you why they think it is good to have friends.

Followup

Have the children draw pictures of their friends. Then have each child dictate a sentence or two about his or her friend. Read the sentence or sentences back to the child as you point to each word.

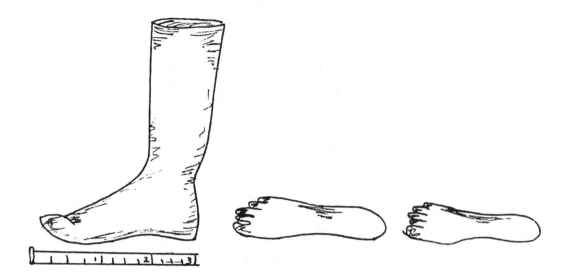

Myller, Rolf. *HOW BIG IS A FOOT?*
New York: Atheneum, 1972
A king decides to have a bed made for the queen. However, when the king uses
his own feet as a measurement, the bed is the wrong size.

Before You Read

Ask the children the question, "How big is a 'foot'?" After you listen to their responses, tell them that you will read a story called *How Big Is a Foot?*

After You Read

Briefly review the story with the children. Ask them why the first bed was the wrong size. Discuss with the children the idea of measuring things, like clothing, to see that they fit.

Let the children experiment measuring distances in the room using their feet. Ask the children if they think all their measurements will be the same. Point out why they will not. Introduce the idea of standard measure, which makes it possible to agree on distances.

Steig, William. *BRAVE IRENE*
New York: Farrar, Straus & Giroux, 1986
Irene's mother has made a ball gown for the duchess, but is too ill to deliver it.
Irene puts her mother to bed and volunteers to go out in a terrible snowstorm
to deliver the gown. On the way, Irene battles the wind which tries to blow the
dress away, but eventually she does get to the duchess's house and returns home
with a doctor for her mother.

Before You Read

Ask the children if they know what it means to be brave. Ask them to give examples of bravery and discuss the concept. Then tell them that you will read them a story entitled *Brave Irene*.

After You Read

Ask the children if they think Irene was brave and if so, why. Ask if they have ever done something that was difficult, in order to help another person. Talk about good deeds that people do for others without expectation of reward. Help the children to develop the concept of bravery.

Followup

You may wish to tape the children's version of the story and play it back to them as you show the corresponding pictures, or perhaps record their stories of bravery and replay them.

Wells, Rosemary. *FOREST OF DREAMS*
New York: Dial Books (division of E. P. Dutton), 1988
This is a beautifully illustrated book, written in rhyme, about the wonderful
things in nature that God has given to a little girl. The story features scenes
from the forest.

Before You Read

Tell the children that this book begins in winter when a child is finding wonderful things in the forest. Ask them to listen and look carefully at the pictures as the story is read.

After You Read

Ask the children to recall some of the things that the little girl in the story saw. Ask the children if they have ever been in a forest or woods and seen similar things. Have the children discuss their own experiences. Then talk about the differences in what they might see in the winter versus the spring. Discuss how the appearance of the forest might change.

Followup

Paint pictures or make collages of the woods in winter and spring. Make lists of things found in the woods in winter but not in spring.

Spier, Peter. *BORED — NOTHING TO DO*
New York: Doubleday, 1978
Two boys have nothing to do on a bright sunny afternoon. They decide to take parts from many different items found around the house and build an airplane. They fly the plane over their house and their parents see them and also all of the things that they have taken apart. In the end their parents make them repair the items and go to their room.

Before You Read

Ask the children if there have ever been times when they just don't know what to do or play. Ask if they sometimes make up new games or build things from boxes and junk. Ask if they know the meaning of the word *bored*. Discuss the concept briefly, then tell them the title of the book that you are going to read.

After You Read

Discuss where the boys got the materials to build the plane. Do the children think that the parents were really angry with the boys for building the plane? What makes them think that the parents were not angry (a kiss and a spanking at the landing and the father calling the boys clever)? Talk about the things that the children in the class have built. Do the children think that this story could really happen, or is it fantasy? Ask the children to explain their reasons.

Teacher Resources: Language Development

Burrows, Alvina T. *THEY ALL WANT TO WRITE: WRITTEN ENGLISH IN THE ELEMENTARY SCHOOL*
Hamden, Conn.: Shoestring, 1982
Developing written language.

Petty, Walter R.; Petty, Dorothy C.; and Marjorie F. Becking. *EXPERIENCES IN LANGUAGE: TOOLS AND TECHNIQUES FOR LANGUAGE ARTS METHODS,* 4th ed.
Boston: Allyn & Bacon, 1984
A description of the various areas of the language arts with chapters on working with special children and children who do not speak English.

Tiedt, Sidney W., and Iris M. Tiedt. *LANGUAGE ARTS ACTIVITIES FOR THE CLASS-ROOM*
Boston: Allyn & Bacon, 1978
The authors stress the need for a positive, active approach to teaching language skills. Practical ideas for assisting skill development are presented.

Children's Books: Language Development

Ahlberg, Janet, and Allan Ahlberg. *THE JOLLY POSTMAN OR OTHER PEOPLE'S LETTERS*
Boston: Little, Brown, 1986
The jolly postman goes from place to place delivering letters to storybook characters such as the three bears, the occupant of the gingerbread house, and so on. Between the pages are envelopes containing the letters. Humorous and fun to read.

Charlip, Remy. *FORTUNATELY*
New York: Macmillan, 1964; reprint, 1985
A humorous story about a surprise party which illustrates the concept of good fortune.

Dr. Seuss. *ONE FISH, TWO FISH, RED FISH, BLUE FISH*
New York: Random House, 1966; paperback and cassette, 1987
A Seuss book of funny characters which helps develop a number of color concepts.

Goodall, John S. *THE MIDNIGHT ADVENTURES OF KELLY, DOT, AND ESMERALDA*
New York: Macmillan, 1973
Picture story of a doll and a teddy bear who awaken to a world of make-believe at midnight and walk through a framed picture to adventure. They return to their original positions at 1 a.m. (Small format is unsuitable for large groups.)

Handford, Martin. *WHERE'S WALDO?*
Boston: Little, Brown, 1987
Waldo is on a trip around the world. He sends postcards from different places describing where he is and where he is hidden within the corresponding pictures.

Hoban, Tana. *CIRCLES, TRIANGLES AND SQUARES*
New York: Macmillan, 1974
A picture book illustrating geometric shapes using photographs.

Hoban, Tana. *COUNT AND SEE*
New York: Macmillan, 1972
A concept book using photographs to illustrate number.

Hoban, Tana. *OVER, UNDER AND THROUGH: AND OTHER SPATIAL CONCEPTS*
New York: Macmillan, 1973
A concept book using photographs of children to illustrate relational concepts.

Hoban, Tana. *PUSH PULL, EMPTY FULL: A BOOK OF OPPOSITES*
New York: Macmillan, 1972; paperback, 1976
Illustrated with black-and-white photographs and single-word captions to indicate the concept of opposites.

Krahn, Fernando. *APRIL FOOLS*
New York: E. P. Dutton, 1974
A wordless picture book in which two children construct a monster head on a stick to scare people. When they are discovered, the monster becomes part of a parade.

Krahn, Fernando. *THE MYSTERY OF THE GIANT'S FOOTPRINTS*
New York: E. P. Dutton, 1977
Children discover strange footprints in the snow and follow them. Their parents organize a search party to find the children when it is feared they are lost. (Small format makes it unsuitable for large groups.)

Lionni, Leo. *ON MY BEACH THERE ARE MANY PEBBLES*
New York: Astor-Honor, 1961
A story about the many different kinds and shapes of pebbles on the beach.

Wells, Rosemary. *MORRIS'S DISAPPEARING BAG: A CHRISTMAS STORY*
New York: Dial Press, 1975; paperback, 1978
Morris, a young rabbit, thinks his brother's and sisters' Christmas presents are wonderful, but they will not let him even touch them. They say he is too young to play with a hockey outfit, beauty kit, and chemistry set. When his brother and sisters discover that Morris has a disappearing bag, however, they are more than willing to let him play with their gifts in exchange for a turn at becoming invisible.

MUSIC, MOVEMENT, GAMES

Music, movement activities, and games offer young children opportunities to express themselves and have fun in a group situation. Many children's stories, picture books, and nursery rhymes can be easily related to songs and movement, and may also suggest games. All of these activities can motivate children to learn. The activities in this section may help develop such skills as sequencing, memory, and muscular control. Music skills include the abilities to distinguish long and short notes, differences in beat, loud and soft tones, and high and low pitches.

Some of the books listed in this section are "story-songs." Such a book can be read as a story and taught as a song. An example of this kind of book is Chris Conover's *Six Little Ducks* (Thomas Y. Crowell, 1976). The musical accompaniment and the words for the song are printed in the book.

Other books in this section lend themselves well to music or movement expression, and specific songs or activities are suggested. You will find that many of the children's literary experiences can be enriched by extending them through song.

Teaching a Song

When you are teaching children a new song, it is important to give them an opportunity to hear the entire song first. You may wish to sing the entire song while the children listen, or play a recording if one is available.

Song charts can be helpful in introducing and teaching a song, and examples are provided for some of the activities. The words to the new song may be printed on chart paper or poster board in approximately 2-inch-high letters. Some of the words in the song may be replaced by a rebus, or picture, to provide clues to assist nonreaders in using the charts. Prereading and reading skills may be subtly taught through the use of song charts.

After the children have heard the entire song, you may wish to sing it again using the chart. Show the children the chart and read the song's title while pointing to each word. Encourage the children to repeat the title with you, as you underscore each word with your hand. Next, read each line separately. After reading and underscoring a line, ask the children to "read" with you. Have the children repeat the line you have just spoken as you point to the words and say the words with them.

After the first verse has been "read" through with the children, ask them to listen as you sing and point to the words of the first line. Give the children a starting pitch. This may be done by singing the first word or syllable of the line. Signal the children to begin singing with you as you point to the words and pictures on the chart. Repeat this procedure for each line in the verse.

At the end of the verse, ask the childen if they think they can sing the whole verse together. If they appear ready, give the beginning pitch and signal to start. Sing with them, and use the chart. If necessary, repeat the words of the verse again, before singing it all the way through.

If the words of the various verses are very similar, you may go on to teach additional verses during the same session. If not, practice the first verse on succeeding days, until the children know it well. Then proceed to other verses of the song. Intermix the teaching of new songs with the singing of familiar ones so that the children develop a repertoire of songs and musical experiences.

Accompaniment

The autoharp, guitar, or resonator bells are excellent instruments for use with children's singing. These instruments provide a pleasant musical accompaniment while not overpowering young voices. The autoharp and bells are instruments that children can be taught to play successfully. Child-made rhythm instruments such as shaker boxes or hand drums may also provide motivation, a chance to participate, and accompaniment.

Activities

Aliki. *HUSH LITTLE BABY: A FOLK LULLABY*
Englewood Cliffs, N.J.: Prentice-Hall, 1968
An illustrated version of the song "Hush Little Baby," with the words and
music in the back of the book.

Before You Read

Tell the children that the story you will read is very old and is meant to be told or sung to young children. Tell the children that they may have heard the words of the song before. Point out that we are not sure who the author is.

After You Read

Tell the children that you will sing the song for them that the mother in the story sang for her child. You may wish to use an autoharp or guitar to accompany your singing, or use rocking motions with your arms.

After you have sung the song for the children, ask them how a lullaby is sung: loudly or softly? Why? Discuss how a song can be used to lull a baby to sleep. Then teach the children the song. Encourage them to sing softly. They may also want to make rocking motions with their arms as they sing.

Balian, Lorna. *THE AMINAL*
Nashville, Tenn.: Abingdon Press, 1972; paperback, 1985
While having a picnic by himself, Patrick finds and catches an animal he
decides to make his friend. Patrick describes his "Aminal" to another child,
but does not tell what it is. Rumors about the "Aminal" grow until Patrick's
friends fear for his safety. When they rush to protect him, they discover that
the "Aminal" is a little turtle.

Before You Read

Ask the children if any of them has a pet. Discuss briefly any pets the children might have. Then tell the children that you will read a story about a pet.

Begin reading the story to the children as you display the illustrations. When Patrick describes the pet to Molly, tell the children to pay close attention. Show the page where Molly is visualizing the pet. Ask the

children if they know what that animal is. Be sure the children understand that the animal shown is what Molly has pictured in her mind from Patrick's description.

When Molly tells Calvin about the pet, the description changes. If the children do not realize this, go back and reread the descriptions so they realize the difference.

After You Read

Discuss with the children the reasons why the description changed from child to child. Then tell them that you will teach them a game called "Rumor," in which they will have the chance to pass an idea among themselves.

Tell the children that you will whisper a message to one child. (A description works well, such as "I have a bird that is blue and yellow, eats cornflakes, and is as big as a cat.") Then that child should whisper what he or she *thinks* you said to the next child in the circle. The message should continue around the circle. The last child will then tell the class what he or she heard. Then compare what the last child heard with what the first child heard. Discuss how much the rumor has changed. Discuss the concept of *rumor* with the children.

Followup

Have the children draw pictures of unusual pets. Make a bulletin-board display of the pictures.

Sabin, Francene. *THE AMAZING WORLD OF ANTS*
Mahwah, N.J.: Troll, 1982
This is a simply written informational book about ants. The illustrations are large and colorfully drawn and dominate the pages.

Materials

• song chart of "Ants Go Marching" (see appendix D, page 146)

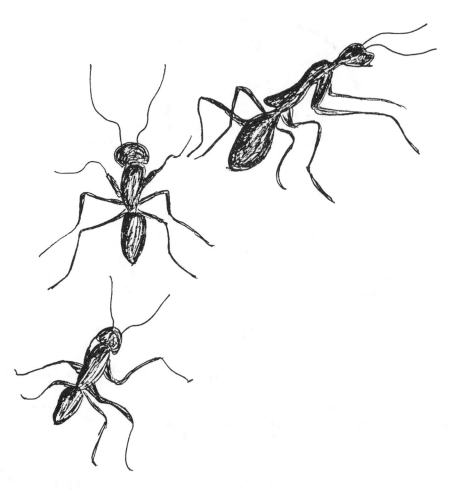

Before You Read

Familiarize yourself with one of the "Ants Go Marching" songs before reading the book. Then introduce the book by using a riddle. For example, you might tell the children that the book you are going to read is about very small animals. Give the children hints that will help them identify the animals, such as, "They make their homes in the ground," "They work very hard," "They have six legs," and so forth. When using this riddle approach to motivate interest in the book, be sure to keep the book cover out of sight until the riddle is solved.

After You Read

Ask the children what new things they learned about ants. Discuss where ants live, their jobs, and other information contained in the book. Then ask the children if they recall the very start of the book when it said, "There are long lines of ants marching right to our food." Ask if they have ever seen those long lines of ants marching along.

Tell the children that you will teach them a song about ants. Refer to the song chart on page 146. You may wish to follow the procedures for introducing a song suggested at the beginning of this chapter. Since "Ants Go Marching" is an easy song, the children can probably be taught the entire song in one lesson.

If you are teaching the second version of the song (page 146), hand motions to match the words are appropriate. For example, display the numbers with your fingers, point toward the sun, pretend to gather sticks, look at your watch to check the time, and so forth. Whenever you sing "hurrah," you can raise your arms in a cheer.

After teaching the children to sing the song, you may wish to have the children form a circle. Everyone sings the first version of the song, while one child marches around the outside of the circle. He or she chooses a second child to follow as the rest of the children sing "The ants are marching two by two...." The song game continues in this fashion until ten children are marching around the outside of the circle. The marching children should follow the leader who may choose to weave in and out of the other children.

Friedrich, Priscilla, and Otto Friedrich. *THE EASTER BUNNY THAT OVERSLEPT*
New York: Lothrop, Lee & Shepard, 1957; 1983
Rainy weather causes the Easter Bunny to oversleep. The Easter Bunny fails to arrive on Easter, and tries to deliver eggs on other holidays, but without success.

Materials

- song chart of "Little Bunny," (see appendix D, page 147)

Before You Read

Tell the children that you will read them a story about the Easter Bunny and a problem that occurs one Easter.

After You Read

Ask the children to tell you which holidays the Easter Bunny arrived for and what happened each time. Ask the children to try to tell you which holiday came first after Easter, which came next, and so forth.

Tell the children that you will teach them a song about the Easter Bunny. Refer to the song chart of "Little Bunny" on page 147. You may wish to follow the procedures for introducing a song suggested at the beginning of this chapter. Dramatize the song by selecting one child to play the part of the bunny. The child who portrays the bunny should pretend to sleep, then begin hopping and giving out make-believe eggs. Have all the children hop to the last five words of the song.

Followup

Design Easter eggs using various colors of paper cut in egg shapes of various sizes. Let the children decorate them with crayons, paint, or glued-on materials.

Funk, Tom. *I READ SIGNS*
New York: Holiday House, 1962; Greenwillow Books, 1983
Peter has learned to read signs. He goes all around town reading signs and then decides to open a sign shop of his own.

Materials

- posterboard or cardboard for signs
- paint or crayons

Before You Read

Ask the children to point out any signs they see in the classroom. If there are none, ask the children if they saw any signs on the way to school. What did the signs say? Then tell the children that you will read a book about signs.

After You Read

Take the children for a walk around the classroom or schoolyard to look for signs. When you find a sign, discuss what it says and why it is there. Look for different kinds of signs. Discuss why signs are important and why some signs have pictures or shapes on them.

When you return to the classroom, have the children set up a sign shop. You may have them make their own signs, or decorate signs you have prepared. You may want to put up the signs around the room.

Followup

Have the children use a large play area to build a "neighborhood" using blocks and boxes. Have them place signs designating parking, railroad crossing, school zone, speed limits, and so forth, in appropriate areas. Discuss the importance of safety signs. You might also introduce traffic lights and discuss their use.

Gag, Wanda. *THE ABC BUNNY*
New York: Coward, McCann & Geoghegan, 1933
An alphabet book with a bunny theme.

Materials

• song chart of "Hop Bunny" (see appendix D, page 147)

Before You Read

Ask the children if any of them has ever had a bunny for a pet. If not, ask if any of them has ever wanted a bunny for a pet and why. Then tell the children that you will read a book about bunnies.

After You Read

Discuss with the children how bunnies move. Ask a child to demonstrate. Then tell them that you will teach them a song during which they can move like bunnies. Refer to the song chart on page 147. You may wish to follow the procedures for introducing a song suggested at the beginning of this chapter. After the

children have learned the song, let them create movements to go along with the song. The children may want to hop, search for food, wiggle their noses, or clean their fur. Variations to the song may include "Skip! Bunny skip!" or "Jump! Bunny jump!"

Followup

Teach the children the "Alphabet Song" to the tune of "Twinkle, Twinkle, Little Star."

Green, Mary McBurney. *IS IT HARD? IS IT EASY?*
Reading, Mass.: Addison-Wesley, 1960
Each of four friends demonstrates things he or she is good at doing, like skipping, hopping, climbing, whistling, and tying a shoe. It soon becomes clear that what is easy for one to do may be hard for another.

Before You Read

Show the children the cover of the book, which shows a child trying to stand on his head. Ask the children if any of them thinks he or she can do that. Tell the children that you will read a book about different things children can do.

After You Read

Ask the children to demonstrate some of the activities shown in the story. Discuss the differences in what children are able to do. Point out that we each have special skills and that individual differences are desirable.

Followup

Make a chart of the different things the children can do. List the children's names and let them mark off the activities they can do as they learn them. Activities might include buttoning a coat, tying a shoelace, skipping across the room, and jumping up and down.

You may also wish to read the following book to the children.

Simon, Norma
Why Am I Different?
Chicago: Albert Whitman, 1976
Portrays everyday situations in which children see themselves as different in their family lives, and yet feel that being different is all right.

Blegvad, Lenore. *RAINY DAY KATE*
New York: Macmillan, 1987
When it rains, Kate cannot go over to her friend's house to play, so the friend has to think of other things to do.

Before You Read

Ask the children what kinds of activities they do on a rainy day. Discuss the kinds of play that one can do if the weather is sunny and then what one might do inside if it is rainy. Tell the children that sometimes the weather can make us change our plans, and that the story you will read is about what happened on a rainy day.

After You Read

Encourage the children to talk about experiences that they have had in the rain. Ask if they were ever in a storm that made them afraid. Ask them to tell you about the different kinds of sounds that are heard during a storm. Then tell the children that they can create the sounds of a storm in their classroom.

Divide the children into four different groups according to their seating arrangement. One group will snap their fingers to make the sound of raindrops. A second group will rub their hands together to create the sound of soft rainfall. A third group will slap their hands against their thighs to make the sound of heavy rainfall. The last group will stamp their feet to make thunder.

Let each group separately practice its sound. Then conduct the storm. Start with the raindrops and add the group sounds one by one. Then have the storm taper off by having the groups stop in reverse order.

Followup

Discuss the good things that result from a rainfall. Talk about the enjoyable things the children can do after a rainfall or on a rainy day.

Read rainy day poems and paint rainy day pictures.

Make a list of rainy day activities.

Display and discuss Peter Spier's *Peter Spier's Rain*.

Janice. *LITTLE BEAR MARCHES IN THE ST. PATRICK'S DAY PARADE*
New York: Lothrop, Lee & Shepard, 1967
Little Bear has an umbrella that can start and stop the rain. He saves the St.
Patrick's Day parade by agreeing to march in the parade and stop the rain.

Materials

- a hand drum
- march record (optional)

Before You Read

Discuss briefly why some towns and cities hold St. Patrick's Day parades and why that day is celebrated. Then tell the children that you will read them a story about a problem that occurred on one St. Patrick's Day.

After You Read

Briefly review the story with the children. Then tell them that they can have their own parade. Using a hand drum, beat a steady rhythm. Have the children begin by clapping to the beat. Next, as you continue to beat the drum, have the children practice moving with the steady beat. Then let one child take the part of Little Bear, beat the drum, and lead the parade. (You may need to help the children keep a steady beat by using sticks or another drum.)

Keáts, Ezra Jack. *THE SNOWY DAY*
New York: Viking Press, 1962; paperback, Penguin Books, 1976
Peter wakes to find the world blanketed in snow and goes out to play in it.

Before You Read

Tell the children that you will read them a story about how a boy had fun in the snow.

After You Read

Ask the children to tell you the things Peter did in the snow. Call on several children to act out the things Peter did. (If the children do not remember, prompt them by showing the pictures in the book.)

Ask several children to lie down on the floor and demonstrate how to make "snow angels." Ask the children what kind of pattern they would make if they rolled over and over down a hill. Have the children demonstrate how they might make other kinds of patterns in the snow.

Followup

If it has snowed, take the children outdoors and let them make designs or stamp out pictures in the snow. Look for tracks in the snow and try to determine what or who made them.

Frost, Robert. *STOPPING BY WOODS ON A SNOWY EVENING*
New York: E. P. Dutton, 1978
This is a very beautifully illustrated edition of this classic Frost poem.

Before You Read

Ask the children to close their eyes and try to think or remember how quiet it is out of doors when it snows. Then tell the children that you are going to read a poem about snow. Read the poem slowly, allowing time for children to view the illustrations.

After You Read

Ask the children whether they believe the person in the poem liked the snow and why they believe that. Ask if they noticed the snow angel that the man made. Have they ever done that?

Write the word *snow* on the chalkboard or chart paper. Ask the children to try to think of other words that begin with the letter *s* (sun, sled, slide, slow, see, etc.). Try making up silly sentences using the words such as, "Suzy suddenly sat on her snowy sled in the sinking sun."

Practice writing the letter *s* on the chalkboard or tracing it in the air. (Remember, if you are facing children and tracing the *s* in the air, you will need to reverse it so that it is not backward for them.)

Ask the children to trace an *s* in the air. Have the children come to the chalkboard and trace the outline of the *s*'s you have drawn. If possible, take the children outdoors and have them trace *s*'s in the snow or sand. You may also want to ask the children if any of them can make an *s* on the floor using a jump rope.

Tell the children that you will teach them a song that has a lot of *s* words in it. Refer to the song chart of "Snow Song" on page 148. You may wish to follow the procedures for introducing a song suggested at the beginning of this chapter. After the children have learned the song, encourage them to think of new verses. Have a few children imitate the snowflakes falling as the others sing the song.

Followup

Use white paint to spatter paint snow pictures on blue paper.

Langstaff, John (retold by). *FROG WENT A-COURTIN'*
New York: Harcourt Brace Jovanovich, 1955; paperback, 1972; reprint, 1988
The traditional ballad about a frog who courts a mouse, and all the animals that get involved in the wedding.

Before You Read

Tell the children that you will read them an old story about a frog who marries a mouse. Point out that the story is also a song.

After You Read

Sing the first verse of the song to the children. Say the words again and have the children repeat them with you. Sing the first verse together. Later, teach other verses of the song. You may want to make a song chart based on the song.

Followup

Make mouse and frog sack puppets for use in acting out the song. Instructions for sack puppets are given on page 74.

Spier, Peter. *THE ERIE CANAL*
Garden City, N.Y.: Doubleday, 1970
Illustrations are accompanied by the words of the song "Low Bridge, Everybody Down" by Thomas S. Allen. The old folk song depicts the active life of hauling barges from Albany to Buffalo and back in the 1850's. Music and historical information about the Erie Canal are included.

Before You Read

Tell the children that you will read them a story about how things were transported or moved around in our country long ago. Discuss the fact that today many things are carried by trucks, but in the past many things were moved by barges, flat-topped boats, along canals. As you read the book, point to the items in the illustrations as they are mentioned in the text. Use the information page at the back of the book to give you more information about the canal which you can relate to the children.

After You Read

Ask if any of the children has seen barges hauling things on rivers or canals. Talk about how the river could float things downstream, but explain that canals needed mules to pull the barges along.

After the discussion, tell the children that you will teach them a song about the Erie Canal. If you have an autoharp, you may want to use it to accompany the singing. You may want to make a song chart based on the song in the book.

Followup

Let children draw pictures of barges on canals or collect pictures of different kinds of boats and ships.

Lionni, Leo. *FISH IS FISH*
New York: Pantheon Books, 1970
When a frog tells tales of the world to a fish, the fish decides to leave its pond.

Lionni, Leo. *SWIMMY*
New York: Pantheon Books, 1963
Swimmy is lonely when his fish school is swallowed, and organizes another school.

Materials

- five small magnets
- five long sticks, or twigs
- string: five 5-foot lengths
- steel paper clips
- colored construction paper
- scissors, crayons

Before You Read

Ask the children to tell you as many ways as they can that fish are different from human beings. Ask them to tell you the kinds of problems they think fish might have. Then tell them that you will read a story about a fish that had a problem.

After You Read

Ask the children if any of them has ever gone fishing. Tell them that they can play a game in the classroom that is like fishing.

Discuss with the children what is needed to go fishing. Show the children a sample fish shape that you have cut out of construction paper. Have the children draw and cut out their own fish from construction paper. For very young children, you may wish to have fish shapes cut out ahead of time and let them color them.

Once the fish are made, attach a steel paper clip at the front end. Show the children how to make a fishing pole by attaching a length of string to one end of a stick or pole. Secure a magnet to the free end of the string.

Designate an area of the floor as a "pond" by spreading out a cloth or arranging a length of string. Scatter the fish on the "pond" and let the children "fish" by attaching the magnet to the paper clips. Encourage the children to use their counting skills as they accumulate fish.

Followup

Create a fish tank bulletin-board display. Have the children cut out fish shapes and decorate them. Cover a bulletin board with blue paper and mount the fish and any other items, such as plants, that the children might like to place in a fish bowl. Cover the display with clear plastic to give the effect of glass. Outline the bulletin board with strips of black construction paper to form the outline of a fish tank.

McCloskey, Robert. *MAKE WAY FOR DUCKLINGS*
New York: Viking Press, 1941; paperback, Penguin Books, 1976
A pair of Mallard ducks decides to raise their family in Boston. When the ducklings are ready to travel, the mother marches them across a busy road to the Public Garden. An understanding policeman stops traffic to make way for the ducklings.

Before You Read

Ask the children to tell you a few ways in which parents help their children. Explain that animal families often behave in the same ways human families do. Then tell them that you will read a story about a family of ducks.

After You Read

Form the children into a circle with everyone squatting and facing toward the center. Choose one child to be "it." The child who is "it" walks around the outside of the circle lightly touching each child on the head and saying "duck." When the first child touches someone and says "goose," the latter must chase the first child around the circle and attempt to tag the first child before he or she reaches the spot vacated by the "goose."

If the child who is "it" is tagged before he or she can reach the vacant space, then that child must attempt to get someone else's space (or go into the center of the circle or "pond," in which case the child who was the "goose" becomes "it.")

If the child who is "it" gets safely back to the space of the child he or she called "goose," then the other child becomes "it" and walks around the circle saying "duck, duck, ... goose."

Nodset, Joan L. *WHO TOOK THE FARMER'S HAT?*
New York: Harper & Row, 1963; paperback, Scholastic Book Services, 1970
A picture story about a farmer whose hat blows away in the wind. The farmer looks for his hat in many places until he discovers that it has been converted into a nest.

Materials

- a variety of hats: toy firefighter's hat, straw farmer's hat, baseball cap, cook's hat, printer's paper hat, and so forth

Before You Read

Collect a variety of hats worn by people in different occupations, time periods, or countries. Discuss with the children the people who would wear the hats you show them. If you cannot find hats, you might cut out magazine pictures to show to the children.

Then tell the children that you will read them a story about someone's hat. Show them the cover of the book and ask them whose hat the story will be about.

After You Read

Tell the children that you will teach them a game using a hat. Have the children form a circle with each of them facing the center. One child is "it" and skips around the outside of the circle with the hat. When the child who is "it" drops the hat behind another child, that child must pick up the hat and chase the child who is "it." If the child with the hat catches the child who is "it" before he or she can get back to the vacant space in the circle, the child who is "it" must try again. Otherwise, the child with the hat becomes "it."

Emberley, Ed. *KLIPPITY KLOP*
Boston: Little, Brown, 1974
Prince Krispen, a knight, goes riding off on his horse. He crosses bridges and streams, rides through grass and over rocks. With each change of surface, his horse's hooves make a different sound. Finally he rides to a cave where he is chased by a dragon. He quickly reverses his journey until he is safe at home at last in the castle.

Before You Read

Familiarize yourself with this story so that you can tell it to the children without having to refer to the book. The book is small in size and the pictures could not be easily viewed by a large group. It is not necessary to memorize the story, and you may wish to make adaptations or add description.

Explain to the children that you and they will tell a story together. The children should watch and listen to everything you say and do. Whenever you use the words that describe the sound of the horse's hooves, dragon's cry, or closing of the drawbridge, the children should echo your words. You may need to demonstrate this process before you start the story. Begin by telling the children the title of the story, *Klippity Klop*. Tell them that when Prince Krispin's horse is just trotting along, it will make a sound like "klip-klop, klip-klop." Demonstrate this by slapping your thighs in time to the spoken word. Have the children do the same thing. When the horse gets to the bridge, the sound will change and you might use mouth clicking sounds, or others. Passing through grass can be done by hands sliding back and forth in a light slapping manner.

Begin the story after practicing with the children on the first sound with, "Once upon a time...." Tell the story with appropriate sounds and gestures with the children assisting.

After You Read

This story may be repeated a number of times during the year. You may want to have a volunteer lead or tell the story later. Children may invent variations of their own. You may wish to display the book in the library center for children to read themselves.

Spier, Peter (retold by). *LONDON BRIDGE IS FALLING DOWN*
Garden City, N.Y.: Doubleday, 1967; 1985
A poem, song, and summary of the history of London Bridge.

Before You Read

Familiarize yourself with the history of London Bridge printed in the back section of the book. Briefly discuss the history with the children. Point out that the real London Bridge was torn down or burned many times and that children made up a singing game about it. Read the poem at the beginning of the book before you begin the story.

After You Read

Teach the children the first verse of the song "London Bridge." Then explain how to play the singing game as follows.

Steps

1. Select two children to be the bridge. Have them stand facing each other holding up one arm each, hands joined, to form the arch of the bridge. The other children skip between them in a line singing "London Bridge is half built up...."

2. The children forming the bridge hold up both arms, hands joined in a double arch, while the line of children skips under and sings "London Bridge is all built up...."

3. The children forming the bridge catch a child skipping under the bridge and gently swing the child in their closed arms, while the children sing "London Bridge is falling down...."

4. The children sing "Take a key and lock her (him) up...."

5. The children forming the bridge take the child who was caught to a makebelieve prison. (Children who are "caught" may return to the group as soon as the game resumes.) Select different children to form the bridge and start the game again.

See Edgar Bley's *The Best Singing Games for Children of All Ages* (New York: Sterling, 1959) for another version of the game "London Bridge."

Lobel, Arnold. *FROG AND TOAD ALL YEAR: "The Surprise"*
New York: Harper & Row, 1976
This Frog and Toad book contains five short easy-to-read stories. This particular story, "The Surprise," is about fall. Frog and Toad who are good friends, each decide to surprise the other by raking the leaves in each other's yard.

OR

Zolotow, Charlotte. *SAY IT!*
New York: Greenwillow Books, 1980
A little girl and her mother go for a walk on an autumn day. They see many things, but the little girl wants to hear her mother say, "I love you."

Material

• song chart of "Autumn Leaves" (see appendix D, page 148)

Before You Read

Talk about the seasons of the year. Help the children to name the four seasons and then focus on autumn or fall. If you are going to read the first book, each story highlights an activity of different seasons of the year. The second book is set in the fall. Tell the children that the story you will read is about something that happens in fall.

After You Read

Discuss the relationship between Frog and Toad. How do they feel about each other? How can you tell? Do you think the friends will be surprised when each sees his own yard in the morning? Why? Talk about how friends help each other.

If you read the second book, discuss the relationship between a parent and child. Is it fun to go walking with a parent? Why? How are parents special to us? Are there ways we can help parents?

Guide the discussion to the time of year. Talk about fall and the special things that you can do such as walking through leaves, piling them up, raking them, collecting them, and the like.

Then tell the children that you will teach them a song about autumn or fall. Refer to the song chart on page 148. You may wish to follow the procedures for introducing a song suggested at the beginning of this chapter. As you teach the song, have the children make motions to match the actions in the song.

Followup

Make torn-paper pictures of autumn trees. Have the children tear a trunk from a piece of brown paper and paste the trunk on a sheet of light blue construction paper. Next, using a variety of autumn colors, have them tear up bits of paper and paste them on the tree for leaves or on the ground near the base of the tree.

Emberley, Ed. *DRUMMER HOFF*
Englewood Cliffs, N.J.: Prentice-Hall, 1967
This is a Caldecott award winner written in rhyme which features a folk
verse about the assembling and firing of a cannon.

Before You Read

Talk about rhyming words with the children. If the concept of rhyming words has been introduced before, suggest two words that rhyme to the children and ask them to supply some others. If the concept is new, mention that some words sound alike at the end. Then give the children some examples such as "new, shoe ... hat, rat." Help the children to hear the likenesses in the words. Then tell them that you are going to read them a story that is an old folk rhyme.

After You Read

Ask the children what Drummer Hoff did. Again reinforce the concept of rhyme by discussing the answer. Then focus on the sequence of events in the story. What was done first in building the cannon? Use the book to illustrate the sequencing of events and stimulate memory. Finally, ask for volunteers to imitate the various characters in the story. As you read the verse, have each person act out his/her role. You may wish to use pretend props. Everyone can make the *kahboom* of the cannon with a hand clap, and then extra children can be the flowers that grow up around the cannon.

After the enactment, you might also wish to talk about cannons of that type being old weapons from long ago and that they are sometimes seen in parks, and other places. You might also have the children look carefully at the figures in the illustrations and notice that one soldier has an eye patch and another a peg leg. Ask the children why they think the illustrator included those things.

Teacher Resources

Bley, Edgar S. *THE BEST SINGING GAMES FOR CHILDREN OF ALL AGES*
New York: Sterling, 1959; 1985
More than fifty games and songs for children ages four through twelve.

Cusack, Margaret, illus. *THE CHRISTMAS CAROL SAMPLER*
New York: Harcourt Brace Jovanovich, 1983
This is a beautifully illustrated book with songs and piano accompaniment.

dePaola, Tomie. *TOMIE DEPAOLA'S BOOK OF CHRISTMAS CAROLS*
New York: Putnam, 1987
A songbook for all ages with familiar illustrated carols.

Dr. Seuss. *CAT IN THE HAT SONGBOOK*
New York: Random House Beginner Books, 1967

Fox, Dan, ed. *GO IN AND OUT THE WINDOWS*
New York: Holt/Metropolitan Museum of Art, 1987
A collection of sixty-one traditional songs with music and lyrics arranged alphabetically with illustrations of treasures from the Metropolitan Museum of Art.

Milne, A. A., and H. Fraser-Simon. *THE POOH SONG BOOK*
Boston: paperback, Godine, 1985
A songbook collection.

Quackenbush, Robert, ed. *POP! GOES THE WEASEL & YANKEE DOODLE: NEW YORK IN 1776 & TODAY, WITH SONGS AND PICTURES*
New York: Harper & Row, 1988

Weiss, Nicki. *IF YOU'RE HAPPY AND YOU KNOW IT: EIGHTEEN STORY SONGS SET TO PICTURES*
New York: Greenwillow Books, 1987
There is a melody line with each familiar tune.

Children's Books

Conover, Chris (retold by). *THE ADVENTURES OF SIMPLE SIMON*
New York: Farrar, Straus & Giroux, 1987
Delightful, colorful illustrations are used to retell this nursery rhyme

Conover, Chris (retold by). *SIX LITTLE DUCKS*
New York: Thomas Y. Crowell, 1976
One little duck leads his friends in merriment as they go to market, cook up a feast, and have a spirited party in this adaptation of an old camp song. Music for the song is included.

dePaola, Tomie. *THE FRIENDLY BEASTS: AN OLD ENGLISH CHRISTMAS CAROL*
New York: Putnam, 1981
A children's Christmas carol.

Ivimey, John W. *THE COMPLETE STORY OF THE THREE BLIND MICE*
New York: Clarion Books, 1987
A story that begins prior to the farmer's wife cutting off the mice tails, and ends happily.

Keats, Ezra Jack. *THE LITTLE DRUMMER BOY*
New York: Macmillan, 1968; paperback, 1972
Picture story of the Christmas song of the "Little Drummer Boy," with music and lyrics.

Kovalski, Maryann. *THE WHEELS ON THE BUS*
Boston: Little, Brown, 1987
A humorously illustrated story of Grandma waiting for a bus. She gets everyone involved in singing the song. The music is included.

Langstaff, John. *FROG WENT A-COURTIN'*
New York: Harcourt Brace Jovanovich, 1955; paperback, 1988
This is the early American folktale with music and story.

Langstaff, John. *OH, A-HUNTING WE WILL GO*
New York: Macmillan, 1974
The illustrated folk song.

Langstaff, John. *OVER IN THE MEADOW*
New York: Harcourt Brace Jovanovich, 1967; paperback, 1973
An illustrated version of the song about the meadow and its creatures.

Langstaff, John. *WHAT A MORNING! THE CHRISTMAS STORY IN BLACK SPIRITUALS*
New York: Macmillan, 1987
This book is appropriate for preschoolers and up. It is illustrated by Ashley Bryan.

Pearson, Tracy C., illus. *OLD MACDONALD HAD A FARM*
New York: Dial Press, 1984
Illustrated for preschool and primary grade children.

Peek, Merle. *ROLL OVER! A COUNTING SONG*
Boston: Houghton Mifflin, 1981
A humorous counting song.

Quackenbush, Robert, illus. *GO TELL AUNT RHODY*
New York: Harper & Row, 1973
Appropriate for preschool and up.

Quackenbush, Robert. *THERE'LL BE A HOT TIME IN THE OLD TOWN TONIGHT*
Philadelphia: J. B. Lippincott, 1974; reissued, 1988
Music and lyrics about the Great Chicago Fire and Mrs. O'Leary's cow.

Spier, Peter. *THE ERIE CANAL*
Garden City, N.Y.: Doubleday, 1970
The illustrations are accompanied by the words of the song "Low Bridge, Everybody Down" by Thomas S. Allen. The old folk song depicts the active life of hauling barges from Albany to Buffalo and back in the 1850s. Music and historical information are included.

Spier, Peter, illus. *THE STAR SPANGLED BANNER*
New York: Doubleday, 1973; paperback, 1986
This version of the national anthem is illustrated by Peter Spier.

APPENDIX A: ART

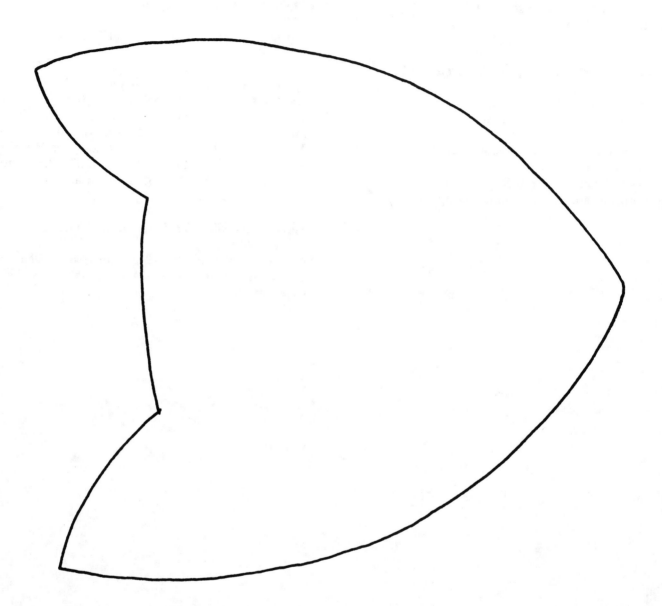

See page 33, sack puppets.

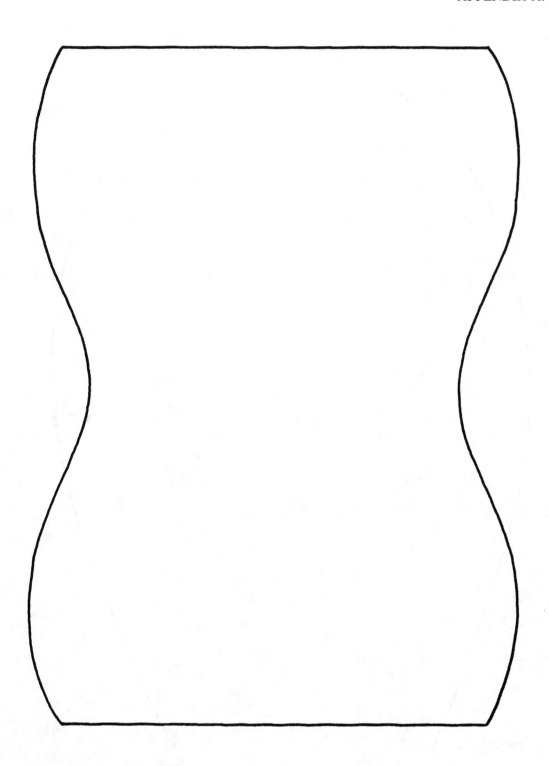

See page 35, clothes pin butterflies.

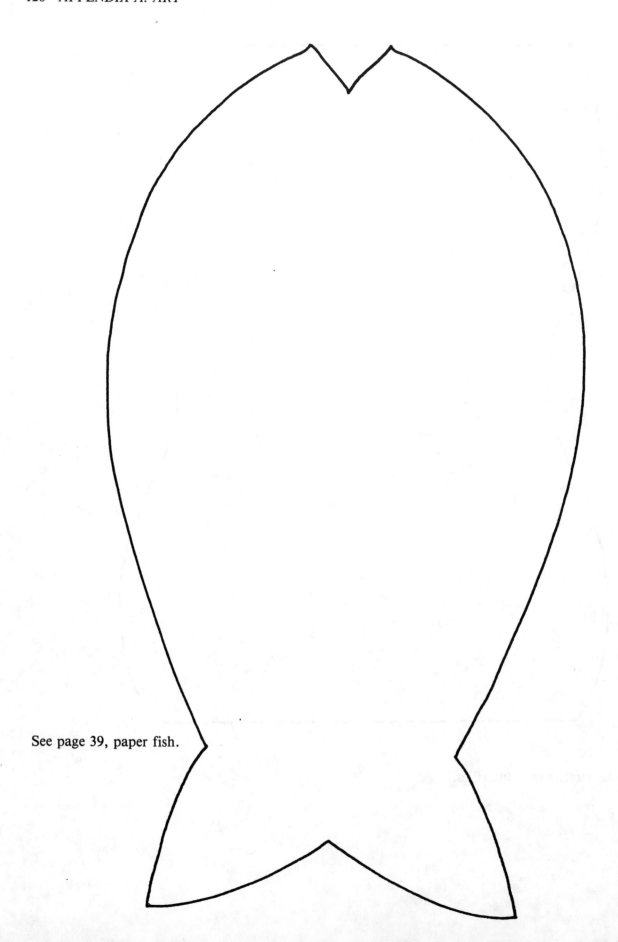

See page 39, paper fish.

APPENDIX B: COOKING

Popcorn
(serves approximately 12 children)
See page 55, popcorn

Use This

½ cup popcorn

cooking oil to cover popcorn

4 tablespoons margarine or butter

salt

Do This

1. Pour popcorn into pan.*

2. Add oil to cover kernels. Top with margarine or butter.

3. Put lid on pan and place over medium-high heat.

4. When popcorn is popped, put it into a bowl.

5. Add salt to taste.

Peanut Butter Yummies
(makes 3 dozen)
See page 57, peanut butter yummies

Use This

⅔ cup peanut butter

½ cup corn syrup

1½ cups graham cracker crumbs

1 cup nonfat dry milk

½ cup powdered sugar

Do This

1. Mix peanut butter and syrup until smooth.

2. Crush graham crackers with rolling pin.

3. Add cracker crumbs and dry milk to mixture.

4. Mix well.

5. Form into small balls and roll in sugar.

6. Serve or chill and serve later.

*If possible, use electric see-through popper. Butter or margarine is placed in the top melt-through holder.

Royal Sandwiches
See page 59, royal sandwiches

Use This

softened cream cheese

small jar of pimientos

green pepper

pitted black olives

bread slices

Do This

1. Use cookie cutters or glasses to cut out different shapes of bread.

2. Spread cream cheese on each shape.

3. Cut pimientos, pepper, and olives in different shapes. Put the pieces on the bread in your own designs. Make stars, plants, animals, faces, anything you like.

4. Display on a platter, then eat.

Gingergread Cookies
(makes 18-20 cookies)
See page 59, gingerbread cookies

Use This

4 cups sifted flour

1 teaspoon baking soda

1 tablespoon powdered ginger

¼ teaspoon salt

1 cup margarine

½ cup brown sugar (firmly packed)

¾ cup molasses

2 eggs

raisins

Do This

1. Preheat oven to 350 degrees.

2. Measure and mix together the flour, baking soda, ginger, and salt. Set aside.

3. Beat the margarine until soft. Gradually add the sugar and cream the mixture. Add molasses, eggs, and beat.

4. Stir in the dry ingredients. Beat.

5. Divide dough among children and form cookies. Use raisins to make faces.

6. Bake for 8-12 minutes until lightly brown.

Applesauce

See page 65, applesauce

Use This

4 apples

¼ cup water

¼ cup sugar

1 teaspoon cinnamon

Do This

1. Wash, peel, and core the apples.

2. Cut the apples into chunks.

3. Measure the water and pour it into the blender.

4. Add the apple pieces.

5. Add the sugar and cinnamon. Replace lid.

6. Blend.

Monkey Sandwiches

See page 67, monkey sandwiches

Use This

bananas

peanut butter

raisins

Do This

1. Peel each banana. Cut bananas in half (one half for each child).

2. Split each piece of banana lengthwise.

3. Spread peanut butter on banana pieces.

4. Sprinkle raisins over the peanut butter.

5. Put two pieces of banana together to form a sandwich.

Butter Frosting
See page 68, cupcake snowmen

Use This

½ cup margarine

2 cups powdered sugar

3 tablespoons milk

1 teaspoon vanilla

1 pinch salt

Do This

1. Cream margarine.

2. Gradually beat in sugar and milk.

3. Add vanilla and salt.

4. Beat.

5. Spread on cake.

APPENDIX C: DRAMA

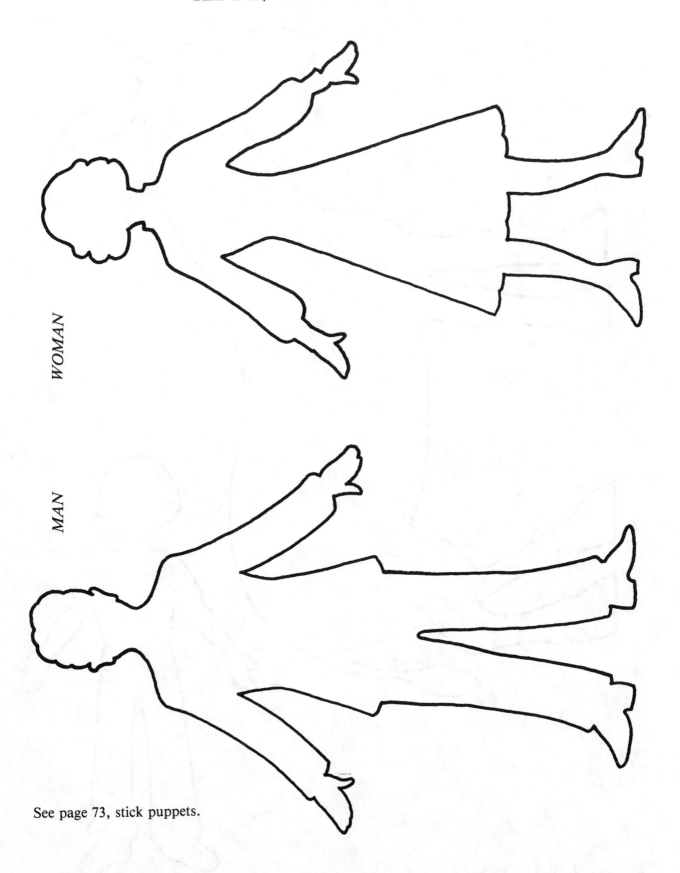

WOMAN

MAN

See page 73, stick puppets.

See page 73, stick puppets.

See page 76, flannelboard figures.

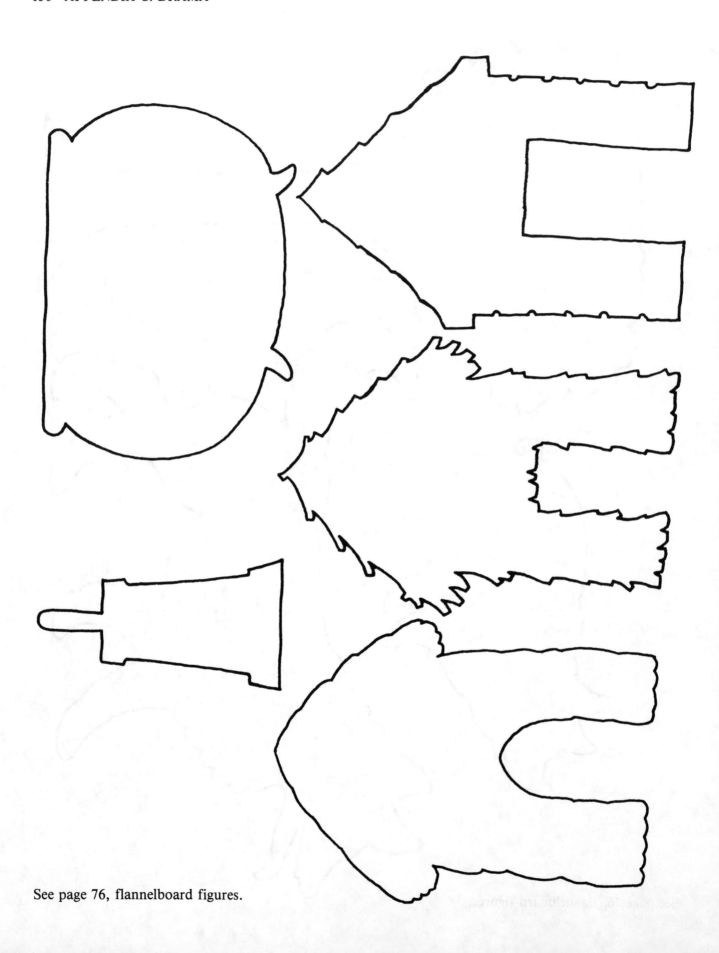

See page 76, flannelboard figures.

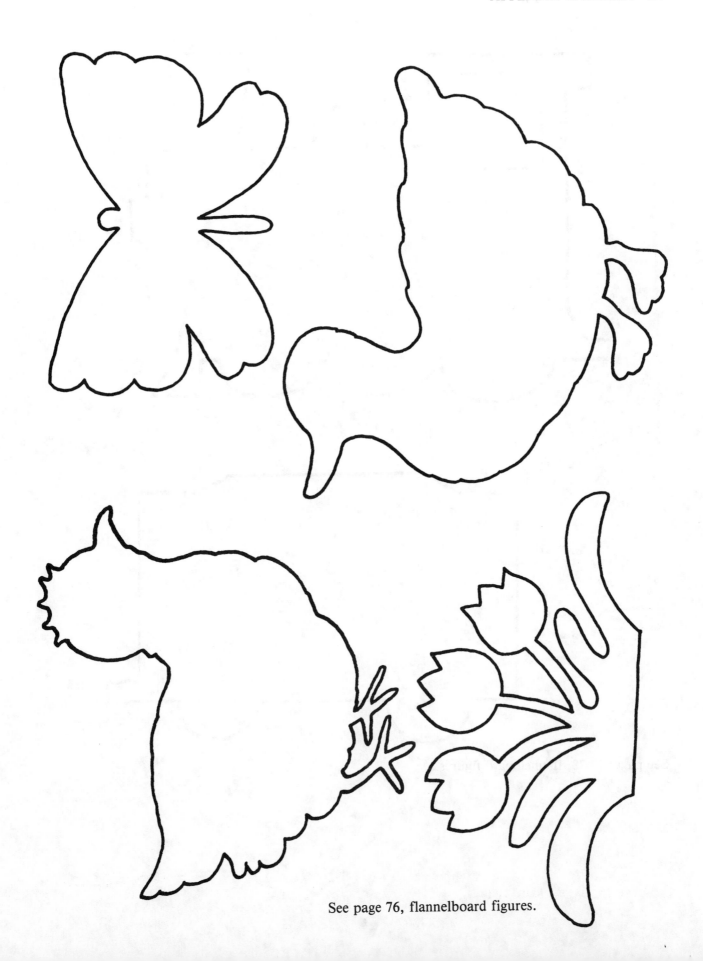

See page 76, flannelboard figures.

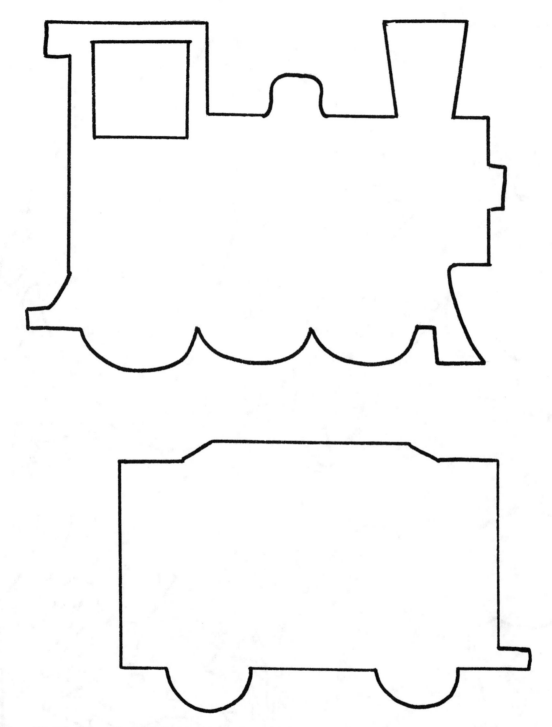

See pages 77-78, flannelboard figures.

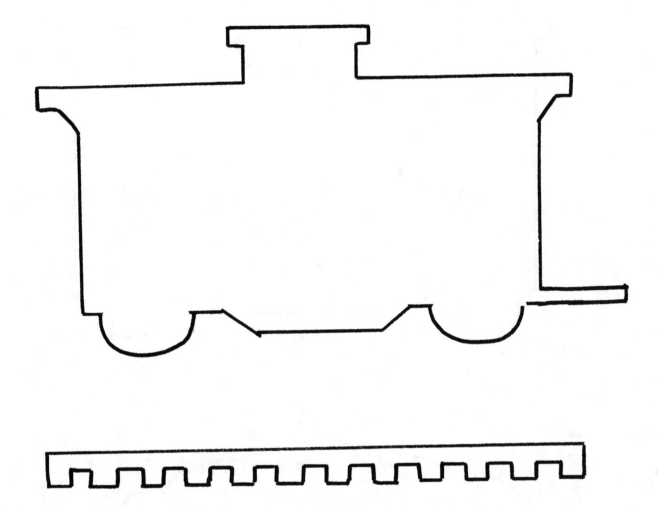

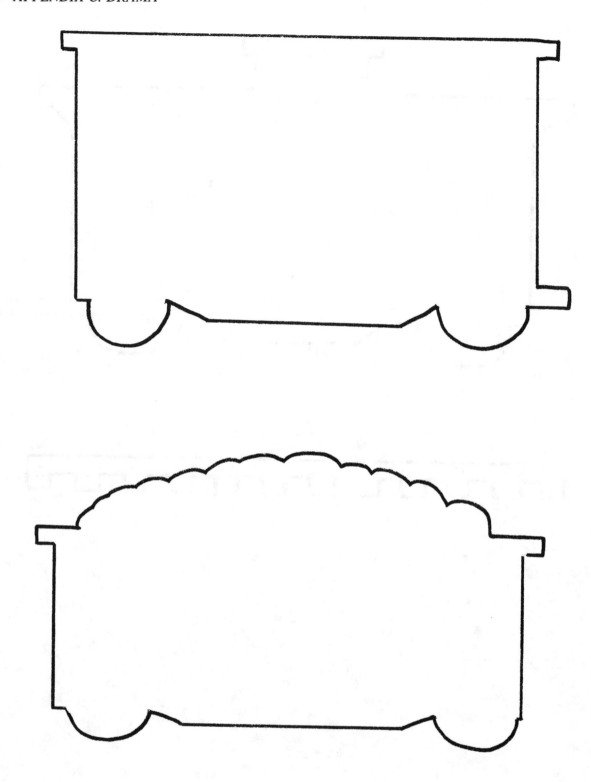

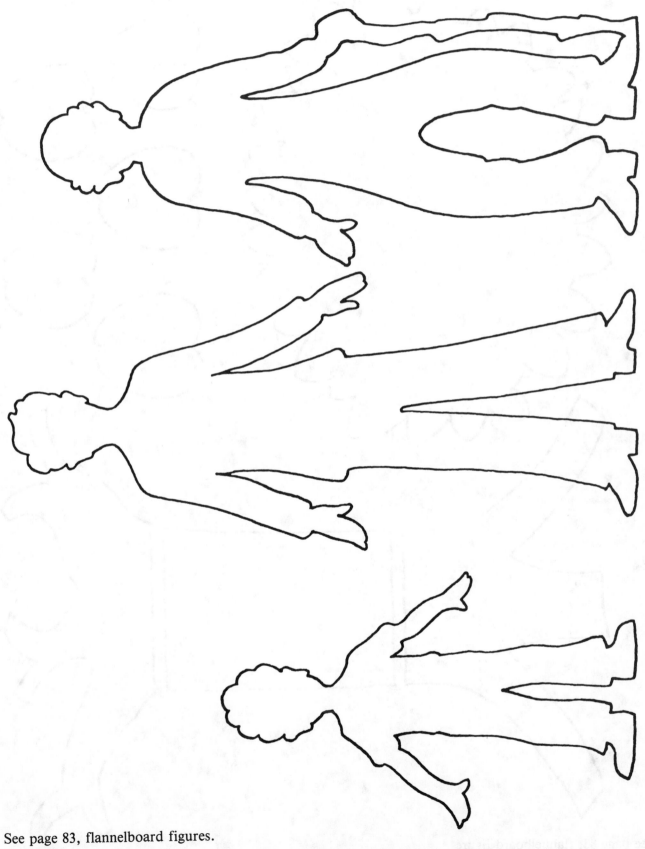

See page 83, flannelboard figures.

See page 83, flannelboard figures.

See page 84, flannelboard figures.

Page 145 is blank.

APPENDIX D: MUSIC

"Ants Go Marching" Song I
(Tune: "Here We Go Round the Mulberry Bush")
See page 107, singing

The ants are marching one by one, one by one, one by one,
The ants are marching one by one, all around the ground.

The ants are marching two by two, two by two, two by two,
The ants are marching two by two, all around the ground.

(Continue up to "10," then go backward to "one.")

Now they're marching nine by nine, nine by nine, nine by nine,
Now they're marching nine by nine, all around the ground.

"Ants Go Marching" Song II
(Tune: "When Johnny Comes Marching Home")
See page 107, singing

The ants go marching one by one, hoorah, hoorah,
The ants go marching one by one, hoorah, hoorah,
The ants go marching one by one,
The little one stopped to look at the sun,
And they all go marching, down into the ground.

The ants go marching two by two, hoorah, hoorah,
The ants go marching two by two, hoorah, hoorah,
The ants go marching two by two,
The little one stopped to tie its shoe,
And they all go marching, down into the ground.

(Continue to "10" using the following verses:)

Three by three: to scratch its knee
Four by four: to close the door
Five by five: to look at a hive
Six by six: to pick up sticks
Seven by seven: to look up at the heavens
Eight by eight: to close the gate
Nine by nine: to ask the time
Ten by ten: to start again

Little Bunny

See page 109, singing

The lit- tle bun- ny slept too long———. He

slept and slept from night to dawn———. Now

he has to hop so fast, giving out

his eggs at last———. Hop, hop, hop, hop, hop.

Hop Bunny

See page 111, singing game

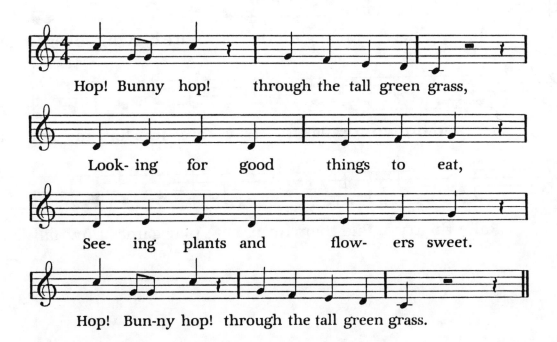

Hop! Bunny hop! through the tall green grass,

Look- ing for good things to eat,

See- ing plants and flow- ers sweet.

Hop! Bun-ny hop! through the tall green grass.

"Snow Song"

(Tune: "Away in a Manger")

See page 116, snow song

The snow is softly falling, it comes from the sky.
It lands on the ground as it falls from so high.
The snow is softly falling, it comes from the sky.
It lands on the trees as I watch it float by.

Autumn Leaves

See page 122, singing

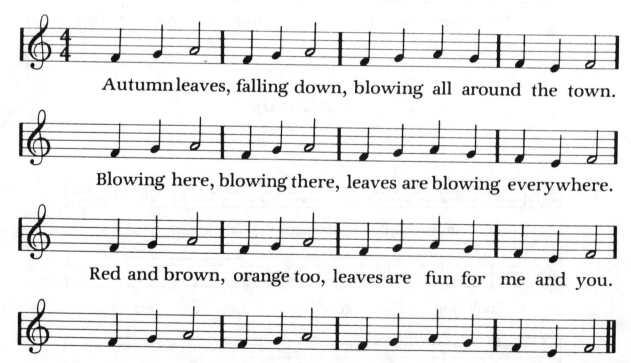

Autumn leaves, falling down, blowing all around the town.

Blowing here, blowing there, leaves are blowing everywhere.

Red and brown, orange too, leaves are fun for me and you.

Rake them up. Pile them near. Let's play games now fall is here.

ABOUT THE AUTHOR

Emilie P. Sullivan is Associate Professor of Teacher Education and Elementary Education Coordinator at the University of Arkansas, Fayetteville. She received a Ph.D. degree and M.Ed. degree in Curriculum and Instruction at Texas A & M University in College Station.

Dr. Sullivan was Visiting Assistant Professor for Curriculum and Instruction at the University of Texas, Assistant Professor in the Reading Center at the University of Southern Mississippi, and has been a reading specialist for bilingual children in the McAllen Independent School District, McAllen, Texas. She has also taught kindergarten, intermediate grades, and junior high school in Texas and New Jersey.

Among the professional organizations of which Dr. Sullivan is a member are the Association for Supervision and Curriculum Development, the International Reading Association, Phi Kappa Phi, Delta Kappa Gamma, and Phi Delta Kappa.

She taught in overseas programs for the University of Arkansas as well as studied early childhood education in the Republic of Ireland and served as consultant to the Arkansas State Department of Education.

AUTHOR/TITLE INDEX

SUBJECT INDEX